Editorial project:
© 2022 **booq** publishing, S.L.
c/ Domènech, 7-9, 2º 1ª
08012 Barcelona, Spain
T: +34 93 268 80 88
www.booqpublishing.com

ISBN 978-84-9936-660-9 [EN]
ISBN 978-84-9936-650-0 [DE]

© Éditions du Layeur
Dépôt Légal : octobre 2022
Espagne, en octobre 2022

ISBN 978-2-38378-028-1

monsa
publications
© 2022 Instituto Monsa de ediciones, S.L.
c/ Gravina, 43
08930 Sant Adrià de Besós, Barcelona, Spain
T: +34 93 381 00 93
www.monsa.com
monsa@monsa.com

ISBN 978-84-17557-57-7

Editorial coordinator:
Claudia Martínez Alonso

Art director:
Mireia Casanovas Soley

Editor:
Bridget Vranckx

Layout:
Cristina Simó Perales

Translation:
© **booq** publishing, S.L.

Printing in Spain

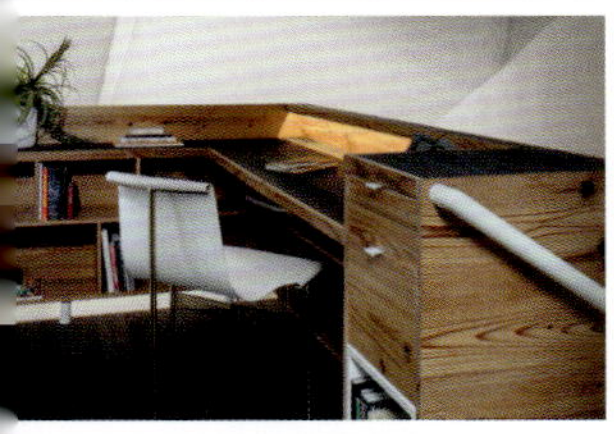

With the COVID-19 pandemic came the abrupt closure of many offices and workplaces around the world and a sudden need for businesses and their employees to work from home or increase the time spent working from home. Kitchens and dining tables were turned into impromptu makeshift workspaces in many a household, while closets, laundry rooms or spare corners were taken advantage of and transformed into a temporary home office.

Many continued like this throughout the pandemic, expecting to return 'to normal' very soon. Instead, coronaviruses came and went; we were plunged in and out of lockdowns; and slowly we began to get used to a 'new normal' and a new era of remote work was ushered in.

The home office design trend took off in 2021 spurring a deluge of interior design articles offering home office ideas and tips, while architects and interior designers the world over saw a surge in the demand for original and productive work spaces in domestic buildings.

There is a myriad of designs in all shapes and size, each adjusting to an individual or family's needs and adapting to the available space. While the basic requirements of a home office are practically the same for everyone, a design may be influenced by a personal requirement, different family structures, a desire to enhance work/life balance, or by the available square-footage or constraints in construction.

For many the home office is here to stay and has become an essential part of the home, encouraging residential renovations and extensions to make space for this new key area, as well as complete make-overs of existing home office spaces, sprucing up the interior, adapting it to current needs or giving it a personal touch.

And, when space is at a premium, extra creativity comes into play, leading to some very original designs, from an outdoor structure giving respite to members of a family of four living in an overcrowded London home, or a central volume which allows the homeowners to 'unpack' different activities as and when they need them – dining, working, sleeping or entertaining.

If home offices are a sign of our times, so are different family structures. From single-parent families to a family of seven, or three families living under the same roof, the home office remains a key feature in each of the scenarios. Inspiring examples abound, such as a home designed for two people wishing to carry out their different routines and activities individually and simultaneously, all the while being connected through clever space planning; or the request to create a chameleon-like space for a single cosmopolitan man, who accommodates his four children two weeks at a time.

In this book, 30 architects and interior designers from around the world share some of their best and most unique home office designs to date, ranging from micro city apartments to medium-to-large suburban or coastal dwellings, from London to Sydney and New York to Mumbai.

Mit der COVID-19-Pandemie kam es zur abrupten Schließung vieler Büros und Arbeitsplätze in der ganzen Welt und der plötzlichen Notwendigkeit für Unternehmen und ihre Mitarbeiter, von zu Hause aus zu arbeiten oder die Arbeitszeit von zu Hause aus zu erhöhen. Küchen und Esstische wurden in vielen Haushalten zu behelfsmäßigen Arbeitsplätzen, während Schränke, Waschküchen oder freie Ecken genutzt und in ein temporäres Heimbüro verwandelt wurden.

Viele taten dies auch während der Pandemie, in der Erwartung, bald wieder „normal" zu sein. Stattdessen kamen und gingen die Coronaviren, es gab immer wieder Sperrungen, und wir gewöhnten uns allmählich an eine „neue Normalität", die eine neue Ära der Fernarbeit einläutete.

Der Trend zur Gestaltung von Home-Offices nahm im Jahr 2021 Fahrt auf und führte zu einer Flut von Einrichtungsartikeln mit Ideen und Tipps für Home-Offices, während Architekten und Innenarchitekten auf der ganzen Welt eine steigende Nachfrage nach originellen und produktiven Arbeitsplätzen in traditionellen Wohnungen verzeichneten.

Es gibt unzählige Modelle in allen Formen und Größen, die sich an die Bedürfnisse von Einzelpersonen oder Familien und an die räumlichen Gegebenheiten anpassen. Während die grundlegenden Anforderungen an ein Heimbüro für alle praktisch gleich sind, kann die Gestaltung von persönlichen Bedürfnissen, unterschiedlichen Familienstrukturen, dem Wunsch nach einer besseren Vereinbarkeit von Beruf und Privatleben, dem verfügbaren Platz oder baulichen Einschränkungen beeinflusst werden.

Für viele ist das Home-Office nicht mehr wegzudenken und hat sich zu einem unverzichtbaren Bestandteil ihres Zuhauses entwickelt. Dies führt dazu, dass Wohnungen renoviert und erweitert werden, um diesen wichtigen neuen Bereich einzurichten, oder dass bestehende Home-Office-Räume komplett umgestaltet werden, um das Interieur zu verschönern, es an aktuelle Bedürfnisse anzupassen oder ihm eine persönliche Note zu verleihen.

Und wenn der Platz knapp ist, kommt zusätzliche Kreativität ins Spiel, die zu äußerst originellen Entwürfen führt, von einer Außenstruktur, die einer vierköpfigen Familie, die in einer beengten Londoner Wohnung lebt, eine Pause verschafft, bis hin zu einem zentralen Volumen, das es den Eigentümern ermöglicht, verschiedene Aktivitäten je nach Bedarf zu verteilen - Essen, Arbeiten, Schlafen oder Unterhaltung.

Wenn Home-Offices ein Zeichen unserer Zeit sind, dann sind es auch andere Familienstrukturen. Von der Einelternfamilie bis zur siebenköpfigen Familie oder drei Familien, die unter einem Dach leben, bleibt das Homeoffice ein Schlüsselelement in jedem Szenario. Es gibt viele inspirierende Beispiele, wie z. B. eine Wohnung für zwei Personen, die ihre unterschiedlichen Routinen und Aktivitäten individuell und gleichzeitig ausüben wollen und dabei durch eine geschickte Raumplanung miteinander verbunden sind, oder die Anfrage, einen chamäleonartigen Raum für einen alleinstehenden kosmopolitischen Mann zu schaffen, der seine vier Kinder für jeweils zwei Wochen beherbergt.

In diesem Buch stellen 30 Architekten und Innenarchitekten aus der ganzen Welt einige ihrer besten und einzigartigsten Home-Office-Entwürfe vor, die von städtischen Kleinstwohnungen bis hin zu mittelgroßen bis großen Vorstadt- oder Küstenwohnungen reichen, von London bis Sydney und New York bis Mumbai.

La pandémie de COVID-19 a entraîné la fermeture brutale de nombreux bureaux et lieux de travail dans le monde et la nécessité soudaine pour les entreprises et leurs employés de travailler à domicile ou d'augmenter le temps de travail à domicile. Les cuisines et les tables à manger sont devenues des espaces de travail improvisés dans de nombreux foyers, tandis que les armoires, les buanderies ou les coins libres ont été mis à profit et transformés en bureau à domicile temporaire.

Beaucoup ont continué à le faire tout au long de la pandémie, s'attendant à un retour à la « normale » très rapide. Au lieu de cela, les coronavirus se sont succédé, nous avons connu des périodes de lockdown et, peu à peu, nous avons commencé à nous habituer à une « nouvelle normalité », ouvrant la voie à une nouvelle ère de travail à distance.

La tendance à la conception de bureaux à domicile a décollé en 2021, suscitant une avalanche d'articles de décoration intérieure proposant des idées et des conseils pour les espaces de bureaux à domicile, tandis que les architectes et les décorateurs d'intérieur du monde entier ont constaté une augmentation de la demande d'espaces de travail originaux et productifs dans les maisons traditionnelles.

Il existe d'innombrables modèles de toutes formes et de toutes tailles, qui répondent aux besoins d'une personne ou d'une famille et s'adaptent à l'espace disponible. Si les exigences de base d'un bureau à domicile sont pratiquement les mêmes pour tous, la conception peut être influencée par des besoins personnels, des structures familiales différentes, le désir d'améliorer l'équilibre entre vie professionnelle et vie privée, la surface disponible ou les contraintes du bâtiment.

Pour beaucoup, le bureau à domicile est là pour rester et est devenu un élément essentiel de la maison, ce qui entraîne des rénovations et des extensions de maisons pour accueillir ce nouvel espace clé, ainsi qu'un remodelage complet des espaces de bureau à domicile existants, pour embellir l'intérieur, l'adapter aux besoins actuels ou lui donner une touche personnelle.

Et lorsque l'espace est limité, une créativité supplémentaire entre en jeu, ce qui donne lieu à des conceptions très originales, qu'il s'agisse d'une structure extérieure qui offre un répit aux membres d'une famille de quatre personnes vivant dans une maison londonienne exiguë ou d'un volume central qui permet aux propriétaires de « répartir » différentes activités selon leurs besoins - dîner, travail, sommeil ou divertissement.

Si les bureaux à domicile sont un signe de notre époque, il en va de même pour les différentes structures familiales. Qu'il s'agisse de familles monoparentales, de familles de sept personnes ou de trois familles vivant sous le même toit, le bureau à domicile reste un élément clé dans tous les scénarios. Les exemples inspirants abondent, tels qu'une maison conçue pour deux personnes qui souhaitent mener leurs différentes routines et activités de manière individuelle et simultanée, tout en étant connectées grâce à un aménagement astucieux de l'espace ; ou la demande de création d'un espace caméléon pour un seul homme cosmopolite, qui accueille ses quatre enfants deux semaines à la fois.

Dans ce livre, 30 architectes et designers d'intérieur du monde entier partagent certains de leurs meilleurs et plus uniques designs de bureaux à domicile à ce jour, allant de micro-appartements urbains à des habitations suburbaines ou côt ères de moyenne ou grande envergure, de Londres à Sydney et de New York à Mumbai.

Con la pandemia del COVID-19 llegó el cierre abrupto de muchas oficinas y lugares de trabajo en todo el mundo y la repentina necesidad de las empresas y sus empleados de trabajar desde casa o aumentar el tiempo de trabajo desde allí. Las cocinas y las mesas de comedor se convirtieron en improvisados espacios de trabajo en muchos hogares, mientras que los armarios, los lavaderos o los rincones libres se aprovecharon y se transformaron en una oficina doméstica temporal.

Muchos continuaron así durante toda la pandemia, esperando volver «a la normalidad» muy pronto. En lugar de eso, los coronavirus iban y venían; nos sumergíamos en cierres y salíamos de ellos; y poco a poco empezamos a acostumbrarnos a una «nueva normalidad», inaugurando una nueva era de trabajo a distancia.

La tendencia del diseño de oficinas en casa despegó en 2021, lo que provocó un aluvión de artículos de diseño de interiores que ofrecían ideas y consejos para los espacios de oficinas domésticos, mientras que los arquitectos y diseñadores de interiores de todo el mundo veían un aumento de la demanda de espacios de trabajo originales y productivos en las viviendas tradicionales.

Hay infinidad de diseños de todas las formas y tamaños, cada uno de los cuales se ajusta a las necesidades de una persona o familia y se adapta al espacio disponible. Aunque los requisitos básicos de una oficina en casa son prácticamente los mismos para todo el mundo, el diseño puede estar influenciado por una necesidad personal, por las diferentes estructuras familiares, por el deseo de mejorar el equilibrio entre la vida laboral y la personal, por los metros cuadrados disponibles o las limitaciones de la construcción.

Para muchos, la oficina en casa ha llegado para quedarse y se ha convertido en una parte esencial del hogar, lo que ha propiciado reformas y ampliaciones de las viviendas para dar cabida a esta nueva área clave, así como la remodelación completa de los espacios de oficina en casa existentes, arreglando el interior, adaptándolo a las necesidades actuales o dándole un toque personal.

Y, cuando el espacio es escaso, entra en juego una creatividad extra que da lugar a diseños muy originales, desde una estructura exterior que da un respiro a los miembros de una familia de cuatro miembros que viven en una casa londinense abarrotada, o un volumen central que permite a los propietarios «desplegar» diferentes actividades en el momento en que las necesitan: cenar, trabajar, dormir o entretenerse.

Si las oficinas en casa son un signo de nuestro tiempo, también lo son las diferentes estructuras familiares. Desde familias monoparentales hasta familias de siete miembros, o tres familias que viven bajo el mismo techo, el despacho en casa sigue siendo un elemento clave en cada uno de los escenarios. Abundan los ejemplos inspiradores, como el de una vivienda diseñada para dos personas que desean llevar a cabo sus diferentes rutinas y actividades de forma individual y simultánea, estando al mismo tiempo conectadas gracias a una inteligente planificación del espacio; o la petición de crear un espacio camaleónico para un solo hombre cosmopolita, que acoge a sus cuatro hijos dos semanas seguidas.

En este libro, 30 arquitectos y diseñadores de interiores de todo el mundo comparten algunos de sus mejores y más singulares diseños de oficinas en casa hasta la fecha, que van desde micro apartamentos urbanos hasta viviendas suburbanas o costeras de tamaño medio a grande, desde Londres a Sydney y desde Nueva York a Mumbai.

A&EB

ANNA & EUGENI BACH,
ALBERT CABRER

www.annaeugenibach.com

Anna and Eugeni Bach are the Finnish-Spanish duo behind the Barcelona-based A&EB architecture studio. Their work covers a wide range of disciplines, from architecture and urban planning to interior and product design, with innovation and research as their driving force. Focusing on the end user, A&EB try to find new solutions and alternatives for every project, prioritizing local and natural materials to ensure perfect synthesis of concept, function and beauty. Through innovation and research, the studio tries to find new solutions and alternatives for each project by optimizing both natural and economic resources. Their philosophy is based on teamwork, working as closely as possible with the end user to ensure the best combination of concept, functionality and beauty.

Anna und Eugeni Bach sind das finnisch-spanische Duo hinter dem in Barcelona ansässigen Architekturbüro A&EB. Ihre Arbeit umfasst ein breites Spektrum von Disziplinen, von Architektur und Stadtplanung bis hin zu Innenarchitektur und Produktdesign, wobei Innovation und Forschung die treibende Kraft sind. A&EB konzentriert sich auf den Endverbraucher und versucht, für jedes Projekt neue Lösungen und Alternativen zu finden, wobei lokale und natürliche Materialien bevorzugt werden, um eine perfekte Synthese von Konzept, Funktion und Schönheit zu gewährleisten. Durch Innovation und Forschung versucht das Studio, für jedes Projekt neue Optionen zu finden, die sowohl die natürlichen als auch die wirtschaftlichen Ressourcen optimieren. Die Philosophie des Unternehmens basiert auf Teamarbeit, wobei so viel wie möglich mit dem Endverbraucher zusammengearbeitet wird, um die beste Kombination aus Konzept, Funktion und Schönheit zu gewährleisten.

HANGING DESK

Anna et Eugeni Bach sont le duo finno-espagnol à l'origine du studio d'architecture A&EB, basé à Barcelone. Leurs travaux couvrent un large éventail de disciplines, de l'architecture et de l'urbanisme au design d'intérieur et de produits, avec l'innovation et la recherche comme moteur. En se concentrant sur l'utilisateur final, A&EB s'efforce de trouver de nouvelles solutions et alternatives pour chaque projet, en privilégiant les matériaux locaux et naturels pour assurer une synthèse parfaite entre concept, fonction et beauté. Grâce à l'innovation et à la recherche, le studio tente de trouver de nouvelles options pour chaque projet, en optimisant les ressources naturelles et économiques. Sa philosophie repose sur le travail d'équipe, en collaborant autant que possible avec l'utilisateur final pour garantir la meilleure combinaison de concept, de fonction et de beauté.

Anna y Eugeni Bach son el dúo finlandés-español que está detrás del estudio de arquitectura A&EB, con sede en Barcelona. Su trabajo abarca un amplio abanico de disciplinas, desde la arquitectura y el urbanismo hasta el diseño de interiores y productos, con la innovación y la investigación como motor. Centrándose en el usuario final, A&EB tratan de encontrar nuevas soluciones y alternativas para cada proyecto, dando prioridad a los materiales locales y naturales para garantizar una síntesis perfecta de concepto, función y belleza. A través de la innovación y la investigación, el estudio trata de encontrar nuevas opciones para cada proyecto, optimizando tanto los recursos naturales como los económicos. Su filosofía se basa en el trabajo en equipo, colaborando al máximo con el usuario final para garantizar la mejor combinación de concepto, funcionalidad y belleza.

HANGING DESK

BARCELONA, SPAIN

PHOTOS © EUGENI BACH

The interior of this 70 m^2 apartment in the centre of Barcelona is completely opened up to create space for a new open-plan living, dining and kitchen area. Removing the long corridor and making the most of the high ceilings, both characteristic elements of this early twentieth-century building, A&EB created a wooden volume to house the kitchen and create a mezzanine level for a unique home office and guest bedroom. This quirky home office space is accessed by white metal rungs situated on the side of the wooden volume. The desk hangs from metal wires, which are attached to the apartment's exposed ceiling beams. This creative solution opens up the apartment and allows for different activities to be carried out at the same time within a central space: cooking, eating, working, resting, playing.

Das Innere dieser 70 m^2 großen Wohnung im Zentrum Barcelonas öffnet sich vollständig, um Platz für einen neuen offenen Wohn-, Ess- und Küchenbereich zu schaffen. Durch den Wegfall des langen Korridors und die Nutzung der hohen Decken, beides charakteristische Elemente dieses Gebäudes aus dem frühen 20. Jahrhundert, schuf A&EB ein hölzernes Volumen, in dem die Küche untergebracht und ein Zwischengeschoss für ein einzigartiges Home-Office und ein Gästezimmer eingerichtet wurde. Der Zugang zu diesem ungewöhnlichen Büroraum erfolgt über weiße Metallstufen an der Seite des Holzvolumens. Der Schreibtisch hängt an den Metallseilen, die an den Deckenbalken der Wohnung befestigt sind. Diese kreative Lösung öffnet die Wohnung und ermöglicht die gleichzeitige Ausübung verschiedener Aktivitäten in einem zentralen Raum: Kochen, Essen, Arbeiten, Ausruhen, Spielen.

L'intérieur de cet appartement de 70 m^2 dans le centre de Barcelone s'ouvre complètement pour créer un nouvel espace ouvert pour le salon, la salle à manger et la cuisine. En éliminant le long couloir et en profitant des hauts plafonds, deux éléments caractéristiques de ce bâtiment du début du XXe siècle, A&EB a créé un volume en bois pour abriter la cuisine et créer une mezzanine pour un bureau à domicile unique et une chambre d'amis. On accède à cet espace de bureau inhabituel par des marches en métal blanc sur le côté du volume en bois. Le bureau est suspendu à des câbles métalliques fixés aux poutres du plafond de l'appartement. Cette solution créative ouvre l'appartement et permet de réaliser différentes activités en même temps dans un espace central : cuisiner, manger, travailler, se reposer, jouer.

El interior de este apartamento de 70 m^2 en el centro de Barcelona se abre por completo para crear espacio para una nueva zona de salón, comedor y cocina de planta abierta. Eliminando el largo pasillo y aprovechando los altos techos, ambos elementos característicos de este edificio de principios del siglo XX, A&EB creó un volumen de madera para albergar la cocina y crear un entresuelo para una singular oficina en casa y un dormitorio de invitados. A este peculiar espacio de oficina se accede por unos peldaños de metal blanco situados en el lateral del volumen de madera. El escritorio cuelga de los cables metálicos, que se sujetan a las vigas del techo del apartamento. Esta solución creativa abre el apartamento y permite realizar diferentes actividades al mismo tiempo en un espacio central: cocinar, comer, trabajar, descansar, jugar.

Sketch

Section A

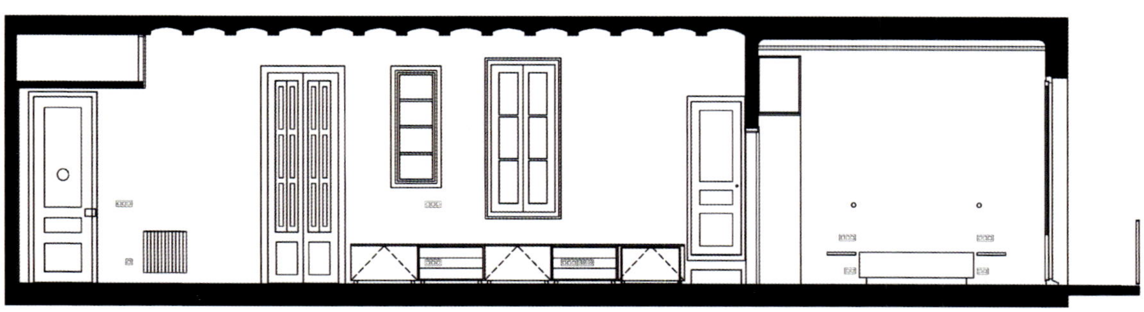

Section B

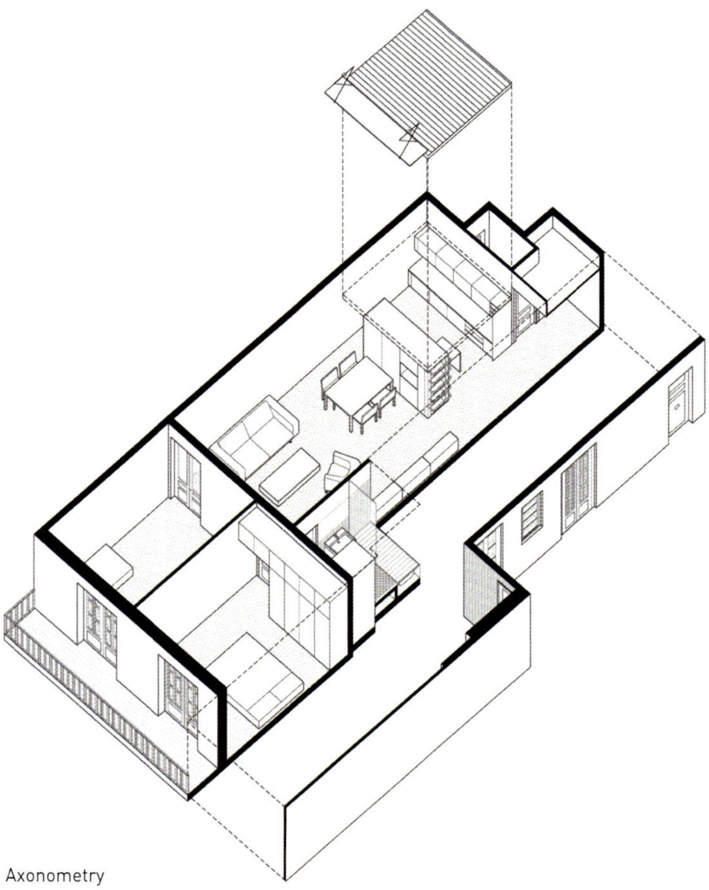

Axonometry

ANNA CARIN DESIGN STUDIO

ANNA CARIN

www.annacarindesign.com.au

Swedish-born Anna-Carin McNamara is the founder and director of Anna Carin Design Studio, a Sydney-based interior design studio specialised in Scandinavian-inspired interiors, imbued with Scandinavian principles of simplicity, functionality and sustainability. For Anna Carin, sustainability is about creating interiors and products that are built to last, free from any trends and fashions. The simple and functional style comes from putting the client at the centre of the design process, thus creating humane and comfortable spaces. Inspired by her native country, Anna Carin's love of nature shines through in all her projects featuring raw materials and a subtle and delicate colour palette. She also applies the 'less is more' principle to furniture and spaces, encouraging clients to reflect on the need for a specific item or room leading to better-planned spaces.

Die gebürtige Schwedin Anna-Carin McNamara ist die Gründerin und Leiterin von Anna Carin Design Studio, einem in Sydney ansässigen Innenarchitekturbüro, das sich auf skandinavisch inspirierte Innenräume spezialisiert hat, die von den skandinavischen Prinzipien der Einfachheit, Funktionalität und Nachhaltigkeit geprägt sind. Für Anna Carin geht es bei der Nachhaltigkeit darum, Innenräume und Produkte zu schaffen, die für die Ewigkeit gemacht sind, frei von Trends und Moden. Der schlichte und funktionale Stil beruht darauf, den Kunden in den Mittelpunkt des Entwurfsprozesses zu stellen und so menschliche und komfortable Räume zu schaffen. Inspiriert von ihrem Heimatland, spiegelt sich Anna Carin Liebe zur Natur in all ihren Projekten wider, bei denen sie rohe Materialien und eine subtile und zarte Farbpalette verwendet. Sie wendet das Prinzip „weniger ist mehr" auch bei Möbeln und Räumen an und ermutigt ihre Kunden, über die Notwendigkeit eines bestimmten Elements oder Raums nachzudenken, was eine bessere Raumplanung ermöglicht.

MOLLY'S COTTAGE

THE CELLIST

D'origine suédoise, Anna-Carin McNamara est la fondatrice et directrice d'Anna Carin Design Studio, un studio de design d'intérieur basé à Sydney et spécialisé dans les intérieurs d'inspiration scandinave, imprégnés des principes scandinaves de simplicité, de fonctionnalité et de durabilité. Pour Anna Carin, la durabilité consiste à créer des intérieurs et des produits qui sont conçus pour durer, en dehors de toute tendance ou mode. Le style simple et fonctionnel provient du fait que le client est placé au centre du processus de conception, créant ainsi des espaces humains et confortables. Inspirée par son pays natal, l'amour d'Anna Carin pour la nature se reflète dans tous ses projets, dans lesquels elle utilise des matériaux bruts et une palette de couleurs subtiles et délicates. Elle applique également le principe du « moins c'est plus » au mobilier et aux espaces, en encourageant les clients à réfléchir à la nécessité d'un élément ou d'une pièce spécifique, ce qui permet de mieux planifier les espaces.

Anna-Carin McNamara, nacida en Suecia, es la fundadora y directora de Anna Carin Design Studio, un estudio de diseño de interiores con sede en Sidney especializado en interiores de inspiración escandinava, imbuidos de los principios escandinavos de simplicidad, funcionalidad y sostenibilidad. Para Anna Carin, la sostenibilidad consiste en crear interiores y productos construidos para durar, libres de cualquier tendencia o moda. El estilo sencillo y funcional proviene de poner al cliente en el centro del proceso de diseño, creando así espacios humanos y confortables. Inspirada en su país natal, el amor de Anna Carin por la naturaleza se refleja en todos sus proyectos, en los que utiliza materiales crudos y una paleta de colores sutil y delicada. También aplica el principio de «menos es más» a los muebles y espacios, animando a los clientes a reflexionar sobre la necesidad de un elemento o una habitación específica, lo que permite planificar mejor los espacios.

MOLLY'S COTTAGE

SYDNEY, AUSTRALIA

PHOTOS © JUSTIN ALEXANDER

Formerly a caretaker's cottage to a large stately home, Molly's Cottage sits at the end of a dead-end street in Sydney's eastern suburb of Woollahra. The project involved reimagining the layout and opening up the roof to reveal trusses and volume that was incorporated into the new kitchen/study/dining room. To make the most of the high ceilings and to avoid any overhead cupboards, a deep row of joinery was introduced along the entry wall. The joinery frames the windows and allows space for an elegant study nook, which is seamlessly integrated to create a neat, classic and timeless space. Built-in cupboards on either side of the workspace hide laundry equipment, a pantry and a fridge.

Molly's Cottage, das ehemalige Cottage eines großen Herrenhauses, befindet sich am Ende einer Sackgasse in Sydneys östlichem Vorort Woollahra. Das Projekt umfasste die Neugestaltung des Grundrisses und die Öffnung des Daches, um den Dachstuhl und das Volumen freizulegen, das in die neue Küche/Arbeitszimmer/Esszimmer integriert wurde. Um die hohen Decken optimal auszunutzen und überhängende Schränke zu vermeiden, wurde entlang der Eingangswand eine tiefe Tischlerreihe eingefügt, die die Fenster einrahmt und Platz für eine elegante Arbeitsnische lässt, die sich nahtlos in einen aufgeräumten, klassischen und zeitlosen Raum einfügt. In den Einbauschränken auf beiden Seiten des Arbeitsbereichs sind Waschmaschinen, eine Speisekammer und ein Kühlschrank untergebracht.

Molly's Cottage, l'ancien cottage d'un grand manoir, est situé au bout d'un cul-de-sac dans la banlieue est de Sydney, à Woollahra. Le projet a consisté à réimaginer la disposition et à ouvrir le toit pour exposer les fermes et le volume qui a été incorporé dans la nouvelle cuisine/étude/salle à manger. Pour tirer le meilleur parti des hauts plafonds et éviter les placards suspendus, une profonde rangée de menuiseries a été insérée le long du mur d'entrée, encadrant les fenêtres et laissant de l'espace pour un élégant coin bureau, qui s'intègre parfaitement pour créer un espace ordonné, classique et intemporel. Des armoires encastrées de part et d'autre de l'espace de travail dissimulent des équipements de buanderie, un garde-manger et un réfrigérateur.

Molly's Cottage, antigua casa de campo de un gran palacete, se encuentra al final de una calle sin salida en el barrio oriental de Woollahra, en Sídney. El proyecto consistió en re imaginar la distribución y abrir el tejado para dejar al descubierto las cerchas y el volumen que se incorporó a la nueva cocina/estudio/comedor. Para aprovechar al máximo los techos altos y evitar los armarios superiores, se introdujo una profunda hilera de carpintería a lo largo de la pared de entrada enmarcando las ventanas y dejando espacio para un elegante rincón de estudio, que se integra perfectamente para crear un espacio ordenado, clásico y atemporal. Los armarios empotrados a ambos lados del espacio de trabajo esconden el equipo de lavandería, una despensa y un frigorífico.

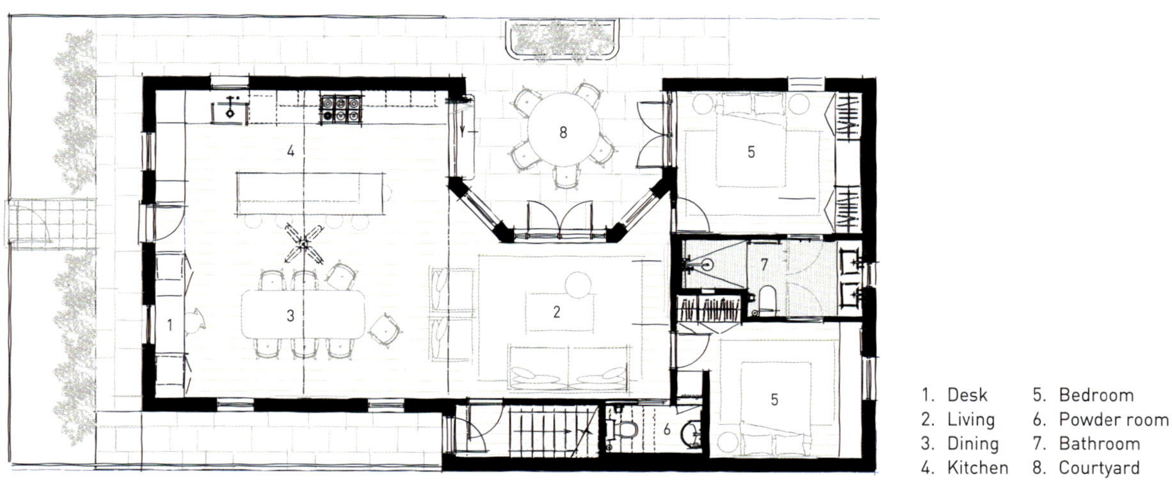
1. Desk
2. Living
3. Dining
4. Kitchen
5. Bedroom
6. Powder room
7. Bathroom
8. Courtyard

Floor plan

THE CELLIST

SYDNEY, AUSTRALIA

PHOTOS © JUSTIN ALEXANDER

The owner of this original 1900's federation bungalow, a cellist from the Sydney Symphony Orchestra, requested a timeless, contemporary and serene home. Working with the interior's generous proportions and high ceilings, Anna Carin Design Studio used a light material palette to contrast the existing darker architecture, highlight the original detailing and create uniformity. A new open layout at the back houses a new kitchen, family room and study space. Placed against a wall and using a floating desk and shelving unit, the smart and functional workspace blends in harmoniously into the heart of this home.

Der Eigentümer dieses ursprünglichen Bungalows aus dem Jahr 1900, ein Cellist des Sydney Symphony Orchestra, wünschte sich ein zeitloses, modernes und ruhiges Haus. In Anbetracht der großzügigen Proportionen und der hohen Decken verwendete das Designstudio Anna Carin eine Palette heller Materialien, um einen Kontrast zu der vorhandenen dunklen Architektur zu schaffen, originelle Details hervorzuheben und eine Einheitlichkeit zu schaffen. Ein neuer offener Grundriss im hinteren Teil des Hauses beherbergt eine neue Küche, ein Familienzimmer und ein Arbeitszimmer. An einer Wand platziert und mit einem schwebenden Schreibtisch und Regalen ausgestattet, fügt sich der elegante und funktionale Arbeitsbereich harmonisch in das Herz des Hauses ein.

Le propriétaire de ce bungalow original datant de 1900, un violoncelliste de l'orchestre symphonique de Sydney, souhaitait une maison intemporelle, contemporaine et sereine. Compte tenu des proportions généreuses et des hauts plafonds de l'intérieur, le studio de design Anna Carin a utilisé une palette de matériaux clairs pour contraster avec l'architecture sombre existante, mettre en valeur les détails originaux et créer une uniformité. Une nouvelle disposition ouverte à l'arrière abrite une nouvelle cuisine, une salle familiale et un espace d'étude. Placé contre un mur et utilisant un bureau flottant et des étagères, l'espace de travail intelligent et fonctionnel s'intègre harmonieusement au cœur de cette maison.

El propietario de este bungalow original del año 1900, un violonchelista de la Orquesta Sinfónica de Sídney, pidió una casa atemporal, contemporánea y serena. Teniendo en cuenta las generosas proporciones del interior y los altos techos, el estudio de diseño Anna Carin utilizó una paleta de materiales claros para contrastar con la arquitectura oscura existente, resaltar los detalles originales y crear uniformidad. Una nueva distribución abierta en la parte trasera alberga una nueva cocina, una sala familiar y un espacio de estudio. Colocado contra una pared y utilizando un escritorio flotante y una estantería, el espacio de trabajo inteligente y funcional se integra armoniosamente en el corazón de esta casa.

THE BERLIN WALL
CAROL EASTON
THE GREAT WAR
LES CARLYON
HARUKI MURAKAMI
RIVALS MICHAEL WHITE
YOTAM OTTOLENGHI PLENTY MORE
TETSUYA
Bill Granger Easy
Maggie Beer
Maggie's Table
THE BOTANIST

THE BERLIN WALL
CAROL EASTON

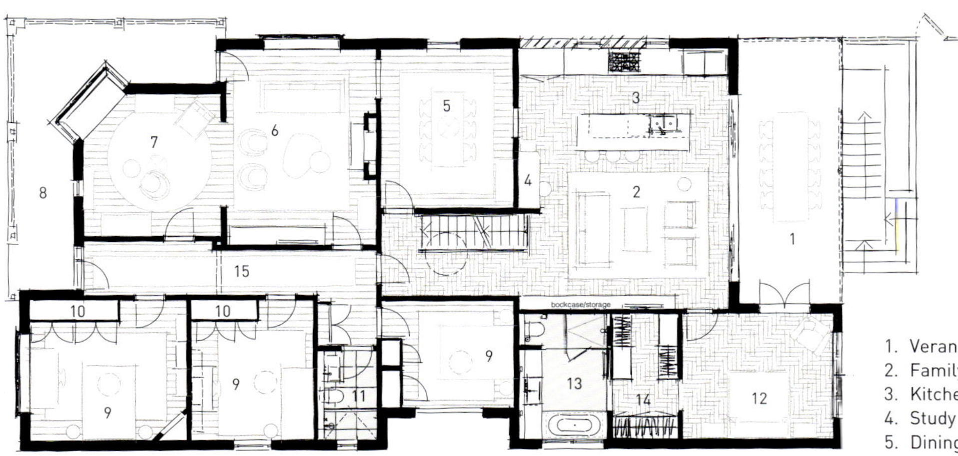

1. Veranda
2. Family room
3. Kitchen
4. Study
5. Dining room
6. Lounge room
7. Music room
8. Front veranda
9. Bedroom
10. Wardrobe
11. Bathroom
12. Master bedroom
13. Ensuite
14. WIR
15. Hall

Ground floor plan

AUSTIN MAYNARD ARCHITECTS

ANDREW MAYNARD, MARK AUSTIN

www.maynardarchitects.com

Austin Maynard Architects explore the architecture of enthusiasm and look beyond the brief to address the bigger picture. They embrace deliberative design and consider a range of issues including liveability, culture, heritage and community connection, as well as mental health and cures to modern isolation. Austin Maynard Architects have a unique approach which allows for a richness to emerge from their work. They treat each project as a singular challenge and work closely with the occupants to ensure they understand their wants and needs. Users are asked to be the authors of their spaces and their city, and are encouraged to draw, research, question and engage. Established by Tasmanian-born Andrew Maynard in 2002 and later joined by proud fellow Tasmanian, Mark Austin, the company's pillars of life, happiness, fun, friends, family, ethics, sustainability and reward for effort, shine through in all of Austin Maynard Architects' playful and edgy designs.

Austin Maynard Architects erforschen die Architektur des Enthusiasmus und blicken über den Auftrag hinaus, um das große Ganze zu betrachten. Sie setzen auf bewusstes Design und berücksichtigen eine Reihe von Themen wie Lebensqualität, Kultur, Kulturerbe und Gemeinschaftssinn, aber auch psychische Gesundheit und Heilmittel gegen die moderne Isolation. Austin Maynard Architects verfolgen einen einzigartigen Ansatz, der es ermöglicht, dass aus ihrer Arbeit ein Reichtum hervorgeht. Sie behandeln jedes Projekt als einzigartige Herausforderung und arbeiten eng mit den Bewohnern zusammen, um sicherzustellen, dass sie deren Wünsche und Bedürfnisse verstehen. Die Nutzer werden aufgefordert, ihre Räume und ihre Stadt selbst zu gestalten, und sie werden ermutigt, zu zeichnen, zu forschen, zu hinterfragen und sich einzubringen. Das Unternehmen wurde 2002 von dem in Tasmanien geborenen Andrew Maynard gegründet und später von seinem stolzen Landsmann Mark Austin ergänzt. Die Säulen des Unternehmens - Leben, Glück, Spaß, Freunde, Familie, Ethik, Nachhaltigkeit und Belohnung für Mühe - spiegeln sich in allen spielerischen und kantigen Entwürfen von Austin Maynard Architects wider.

KING BILL

TOWER HOUSE

Austin Maynard Architects explore l'architecture de l'enthousiasme et va au-delà du cahier des charges pour prendre en compte la situation dans son ensemble. Ils adoptent une conception délibérative et prennent en compte une série de questions telles que l'habitabilité, la culture, le patrimoine et les liens communautaires, ainsi que la santé mentale et les remèdes à l'isolement moderne. Austin Maynard Architects a une approche unique qui permet à la richesse de son travail d'émerger. Ils traitent chaque projet comme un défi singulier et travaillent en étroite collaboration avec les occupants pour s'assurer qu'ils comprennent leurs désirs et leurs besoins. Les utilisateurs sont invités à être les auteurs de leurs espaces et de leur ville, et sont encouragés à dessiner, à faire des recherches, à poser des questions et à s'engager. Fondée en 2002 par Andrew Maynard, originaire de Tasmanie, et rejointe ensuite par Mark Austin, un fier compatriote de Tasmanie, la société s'appuie sur les piliers que sont la vie, le bonheur, l'amusement, les amis, la famille, l'éthique, la durabilité et la récompense des efforts, qui transparaissent dans toutes les conceptions ludiques et audacieuses d'Austin Maynard Architects.

Austin Maynard Architects explora la arquitectura del entusiasmo y mira más allá de las instrucciones para abordar el panorama general. Adoptan el diseño deliberativo y consideran una serie de cuestiones como la habitabilidad, la cultura, el patrimonio y la conexión con la comunidad, así como la salud mental y las curas al aislamiento moderno. Austin Maynard Architects tiene un enfoque único que permite que surja la riqueza de su trabajo. Tratan cada proyecto como un reto singular y trabajan estrechamente con los ocupantes para asegurarse de que entienden sus deseos y necesidades. Se pide a los usuarios que sean los autores de sus espacios y su ciudad, y se les anima a dibujar, investigar, cuestionar y participar. Fundada por Andrew Maynard, nacido en Tasmania, en 2002, y a la que más tarde se unió su compatriota Mark Austin, los pilares de la empresa, que son la vida, la felicidad, la diversión, los amigos, la familia, la ética, la sostenibilidad y la recompensa por el esfuerzo, brillan en todos sus diseños juguetones y atrevidos.

KING BILL

MELBOURNE, AUSTRALIA

PHOTOS © DEREK SWALWELL

Located in the bohemian suburb of Fitzroy, Melbourne, King Bill is the "forever home" of a family of four who wanted more living space without creating a huge home. The renovation of this two-story terrace house dating back to the 1850s, incorporates an empty garden site to the east and an old stable building at the rear. Initially separate lots, a glazed corridor now runs along the eastern outer wall of the original terrace house linking it with the stable and the new pavilion, which houses kitchen, living and dining spaces. The brick-and-metal rear stable was turned into a steel-clad garage, study, and retreat for the parents. The north-facing bedroom and bathroom on the upper level are separated by a large curved sliding wall which opens out onto an open net hanging over the study below. Overlooking the garden, the study receives plenty of daylight while the double-glazed windows ensure it does not get too hot in summer.

King Bill befindet sich im unkonventionellen Vorort Fitzroy in Melbourne und ist das „Zuhause für immer" einer vierköpfigen Familie, die mehr Wohnraum wollte, ohne ein riesiges Haus zu bauen. Bei der Renovierung dieses zweistöckigen Reihenhauses aus den 1850er Jahren wurden ein leeres Gartengrundstück im Osten und ein altes Stallgebäude im hinteren Bereich einbezogen. Ursprünglich getrennte Grundstücke, verläuft nun ein verglaster Korridor entlang der östlichen Außenwand des ursprünglichen Reihenhauses, der es mit dem Stall und dem neuen Pavillon verbindet, in dem Küche, Wohn- und Essbereich untergebracht sind.Der hintere Stall aus Backstein und Metall wurde zu einer stahlverkleideten Garage, einem Arbeitszimmer und einem Rückzugsort für die Eltern umgebaut. Das nach Norden ausgerichtete Schlafzimmer und das Badezimmer im Obergeschoss sind durch eine große geschwungene Schiebewand getrennt, die sich zu einem offenen Netz öffnet, das über dem darunter liegenden Arbeitszimmer hängt. Mit Blick auf den Garten erhält das Arbeitszimmer viel Tageslicht, während die doppelt verglasten Fenster dafür sorgen, dass es im Sommer nicht zu heiß wird.

Située dans la banlieue bohème de Fitzroy, à Melbourne, King Bill est la « maison pour toujours » d'une famille de quatre personnes qui souhaitait disposer de plus d'espace de vie sans pour autant créer une maison gigantesque. La rénovation de cette maison en terrasse à deux étages, datant des années 1850, intègre un terrain vide à l'est et un ancien bâtiment d'écurie à l'arrière. Initialement des lots séparés, un couloir vitré longe désormais le mur extérieur est de la maison terrasse d'origine, la reliant à l'écurie et au nouveau pavillon, qui abrite la cuisine, le salon et la salle à manger.L'écurie arrière, faite de briques et de métal, a été transformée en un garage, un bureau et un lieu de retraite pour les parents, recouverts d'acier. La chambre à coucher et la salle de bains du niveau supérieur, orientées au nord, sont séparées par une grande paroi coulissante incurvée qui s'ouvre sur un filet ouvert suspendu au-dessus du bureau situé en dessous. Donnant sur le jardin, le bureau reçoit beaucoup de lumière du jour tandis que les fenêtres à double vitrage permettent de ne pas avoir trop chaud en été.

Situado en el bohemio barrio de Fitzroy, Melbourne, King Bill es el «hogar para siempre» de una familia de cuatro miembros que quería más espacio para vivir sin crear una casa enorme. La renovación de esta casa adosada de dos plantas, que data de la década de 1850, incorpora un terreno ajardinado vacío al este y un antiguo edificio de caballerizas en la parte trasera. Aunque en un principio se trataba de parcelas separadas, un pasillo acristalado recorre ahora el muro exterior oriental de la casa adosada original, conectándola con el establo y el nuevo pabellón, que alberga espacios de cocina, salón y comedor. El establo trasero de ladrillo y metal se convirtió en un garaje revestido de acero, un estudio y un refugio para los padres. El dormitorio y el cuarto de baño de la planta superior, orientados al norte, están separados por una gran pared corredera curvada que se abre a una red abierta que cuelga sobre el estudio del nivel inferior. Con vistas al jardín, el estudio recibe mucha luz natural, mientras que las ventanas de doble acristalamiento garantizan que no haga demasiado calor en verano.

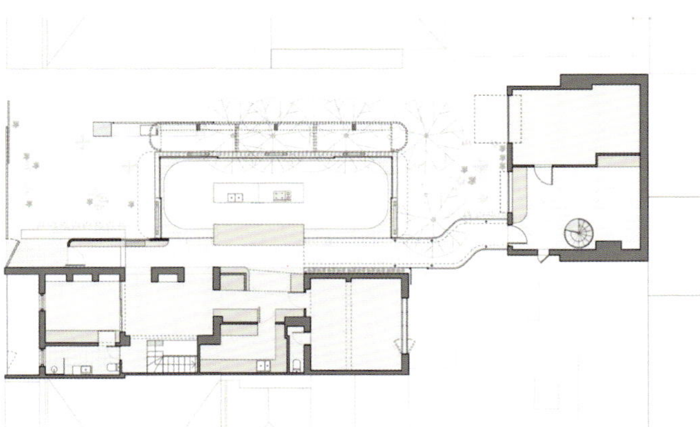

Ground floor plan

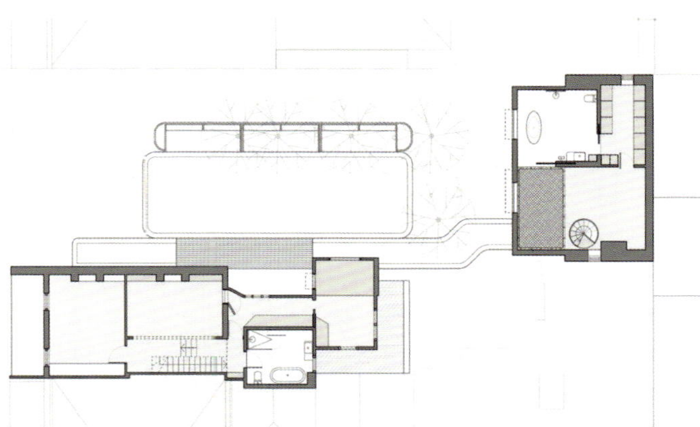

First floor plan

TOWER HOUSE

MELBOURNE, AUSTRALIA

PHOTOS © PETER BENNETTS & TESS KELLY

Located in Alphington, a suburb northeast of central Melbourne, Tower House is born out of the occupants' desire to have a home "for community, art and nature to come together". Following many concurrent discussions with the parents, S+P, and some sketches drawn by their eight-year-old twin boys, Austin Maynard Architects designed a village for this family of four. Designed to inspire the twin boys as they grow and learn, their study area is a wholly vertical space with a bookshelf running from floor to ceiling. The desks are at the base of the studio with a net hanging above the workspace. The net is a place where the boys can read and contemplate the view to the street and backyard. The library designed for S is a place of thought and contemplation. Slightly submerged, the desk is almost buried in the garden. Lined with dark spotted gum the library has an age and a wisdom that is in contrast to the playful contemplation of the boys' study.

Située à Alphington, une banlieue au nord-est du centre de Melbourne, Tower House est née du désir des occupants d'avoir une maison « pour que la communauté, l'art et la nature se réunissent ». Après de nombreuses discussions simultanées avec les parents, S+P, et quelques croquis dessinés par leurs jumeaux de huit ans, Austin Maynard Architects a conçu un village pour cette famille de quatre personnes. Conçu pour inspirer les jumeaux au fur et à mesure qu'ils grandissent et apprennent, leur espace d'étude est un espace entièrement vertical avec une bibliothèque allant du sol au plafond. Les bureaux sont situés à la base du studio et un filet est suspendu au-dessus de l'espace de travail. Le filet est un endroit où les garçons peuvent lire et contempler la vue sur la rue et le jardin. La bibliothèque conçue pour S est un lieu de réflexion et de contemplation. Légèrement submergé, le bureau est presque enterré dans le jardin. Tapissée de gomme sombre tachetée, la bibliothèque a un âge et une sagesse qui contrastent avec la contemplation ludique du bureau des garçons.

Das in Alphington, einem Vorort nordöstlich des Zentrums von Melbourne, gelegene Tower House entstand aus dem Wunsch der Bewohner nach einem Haus, in dem „Gemeinschaft, Kunst und Natur zusammenkommen können". Nach vielen gleichzeitigen Gesprächen mit den Eltern, S+P, und einigen Skizzen ihrer achtjährigen Zwillingsjungen entwarfen Austin Maynard Architects ein Dorf für die vierköpfige Familie. Um die Zwillingsjungen beim Wachsen und Lernen zu inspirieren, ist ihr Arbeitsbereich ein vollständig vertikaler Raum mit einem Bücherregal, das vom Boden bis zur Decke reicht. Die Schreibtische befinden sich im unteren Teil des Studios, über dem Arbeitsbereich hängt ein Netz. Das Netz ist ein Ort, an dem die Jungen lesen und den Blick auf die Straße und den Hinterhof genießen können. Die für S entworfene Bibliothek ist ein Ort des Nachdenkens und der Kontemplation. Der Schreibtisch ist leicht eingetaucht und liegt fast im Garten begraben. Die mit dunklem geflecktem Gummi ausgekleidete Bibliothek hat ein Alter und eine Weisheit, die im Gegensatz zur spielerischen Kontemplation des Arbeitszimmers der Jungen steht.

Situada en Alphington, un suburbio al noreste del centro de Melbourne, Tower House nace del deseo de sus ocupantes de tener una casa «para que la comunidad, el arte y la naturaleza se unan». Tras muchas conversaciones simultáneas con los padres, S+P, y algunos bocetos dibujados por sus hijos gemelos de ocho años, Austin Maynard Architects diseñó una villa para esta familia de cuatro miembros. Pensada para inspirar a los gemelos mientras crecen y aprenden, su zona de estudio es un espacio totalmente vertical con una estantería que va del suelo al techo. Los escritorios están en la base del estudio, con una red que cuelga por encima del espacio de trabajo. La red es un lugar donde los chicos pueden leer y contemplar las vistas a la calle y al patio trasero. La biblioteca diseñada para S es un lugar de pensamiento y contemplación. Ligeramente sumergido, el escritorio está casi enterrado en el jardín. Revestida de goma oscura, la biblioteca tiene una edad y una sabiduría que contrastan con la contemplación lúdica del estudio de los chicos.

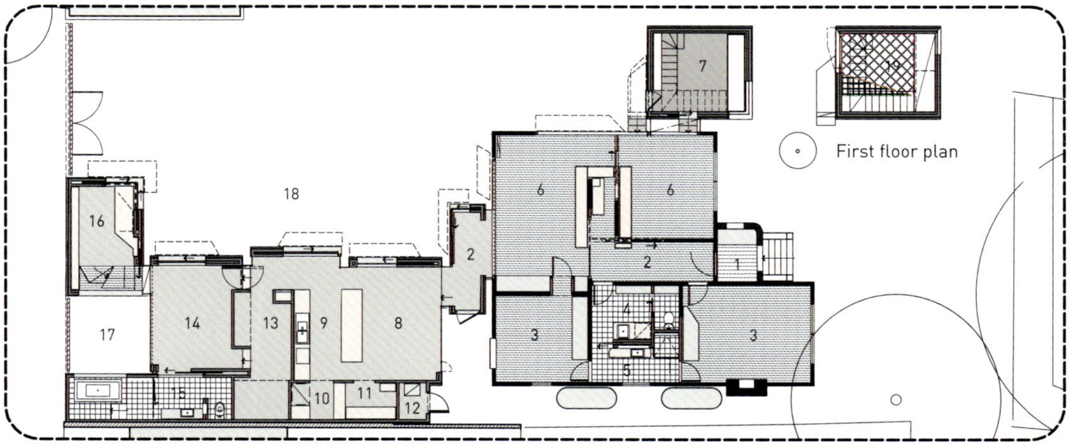

Ground floor plan

1. Entry
2. Hall
3. Bedroom
4. Laundry
5. Bathroom
6. Living
7. Study
8. Dining
9. Kitchen
10. Pantry
11. Store
12. Services
13. Walk-in robe
14. Master bedroom
15. Ensuite
16. Library
17. Courtyard
18. Garden
19. Study net

CRAIG STEELY ARCHITECTURE

CRAIG STEELY

www.craigsteely.com

Craig Steely Architecture has studios in Hawaii and San Francisco and their buildings have been described as unique hybrids of these two places. Exploring the boundaries of integration and emancipation from nature, Craig Steely's projects are singular pieces of architecture rooted in their context, which embrace the realities of the environment and our connection/separation to it. Starting from a classic modern tradition, Craig Steely Architecture is known for its crisp lines and clarity of vision. They like to work with clients who share their enthusiasm for the design process as a truly creative endeavour and the exploration of unique sites.

Craig Steely Architecture hat Ateliers in Hawaii und San Francisco, und seine Gebäude werden als einzigartige Hybride dieser beiden Orte beschrieben. Craig Steelys Projekte, die die Grenzen der Integration und Emanzipation von der Natur ausloten, sind einzigartige Architekturen, die in ihrem Kontext verwurzelt sind und die Realitäten der Umwelt und unsere Verbindung/Trennung von ihr berücksichtigen. Craig Steely Architecture ist für seine klaren Linien und seine klare Vision bekannt und steht in der Tradition der klassischen Moderne. Sie arbeiten gerne mit Kunden zusammen, die ihre Begeisterung für den Designprozess als wahrhaft kreatives Unterfangen und die Erkundung einzigartiger Orte teilen.

D FIN HOUSE

PAM & PAUL'S

Craig Steely Architecture possède des studios à Hawaï et à San Francisco et ses bâtiments ont été décrits comme des hybrides uniques de ces deux endroits. Explorant les limites de l'intégration et de l'émancipation de la nature, les projets de Craig Steely sont des pièces d'architecture singulières enracinées dans leur contexte, embrassant les réalités de l'environnement et notre connexion/séparation avec lui. S'inspirant d'une tradition moderne classique, Craig Steely Architecture est connu pour ses lignes nettes et la clarté de sa vision. Ils aiment travailler avec des clients qui partagent leur enthousiasme pour le processus de conception en tant qu'entreprise véritablement créative et pour l'exploration de lieux uniques.

Craig Steely Architecture tiene estudios en Hawai y San Francisco y sus edificios han sido descritos como híbridos únicos de estos dos lugares. Explorando los límites de la integración y la emancipación de la naturaleza, los proyectos de Craig Steely son piezas singulares de arquitectura enraizadas en su contexto, que abrazan las realidades del entorno y nuestra conexión/separación con él. Partiendo de una tradición moderna clásica, Craig Steely Architecture es conocido por sus líneas nítidas y su claridad de visión. Les gusta trabajar con clientes que comparten su entusiasmo por el proceso de diseño como un esfuerzo verdaderamente creativo y la exploración de lugares únicos.

D FIN HOUSE

CAPTAIN COOK, HAWAII, UNITED STATES

PHOTOS © DARREN BRADLEY

Located near Captain Cook, above Kealakekua Bay on the Big Island of Hawaii D Fin House is features eight columns, which support a curved and exposed glue-laminated wood beam structure creating a 17 m diameter steel clad wood and glass drum. This round structure bends around the panoramic landscape and immerses the occupant into the expansive view of the Kona coastline. Like a classic 60s "D" fin surfboard, a steep roofed loft projects symmetrically from the back of the circle structure below. Oriented towards Ka'u and South Point, the triangle loft space rising out of the wood and glass drum is used as an office by the owner, who can enjoy views of Point Kakio on clear days. Inspired by old Hawaiian single wall houses, the walls and ceiling are made up of exposed pine decking. The pine bookcase is designed by Craig Steely.

Das in der Nähe von Captain Cook, oberhalb der Kealakekua Bay auf der Big Island von Hawaii gelegene D Fin House besteht aus acht Säulen, die eine Struktur aus freiliegenden, gebogenen Brettschichtholzbalken tragen, die eine stahlverkleidete Holz- und Glastrommel mit einem Durchmesser von 17 m bilden. Diese runde Struktur faltet sich um die Panoramalandschaft und lässt den Bewohner in den weiten Blick auf die Küste von Kona eintauchen. Wie ein klassisches Surfbrett mit D-Finne aus den 1960er Jahren ragt ein steil überdachtes Loft symmetrisch aus der Rückseite des unteren Rundbaus heraus. Mit Blick auf Ka'u und South Point wird das dreieckige Loft, das sich aus der Holz- und Glastrommel erhebt, vom Eigentümer als Büro genutzt, der an klaren Tagen den Blick auf Point Kakio genießen kann. Inspiriert von den alten einwandigen hawaiianischen Häusern sind die Wände und die Decke aus Kiefernholz gefertigt. Das Bücherregal, ebenfalls aus Kiefernholz, wurde von Craig Steely selbst entworfen.

Située près de Captain Cook, au-dessus de la baie de Kealakekua, sur la grande île d'Hawaï, la D Fin House se compose de huit colonnes soutenant une structure de poutres en bois lamellé-collé courbée et exposée qui crée un tambour en bois et en verre de 17 m de diamètre, recouvert d'acier. Cette structure ronde se plie autour du paysage panoramique et immerge l'occupant dans la vue imprenable sur le littoral de Kona. À l'instar d'une planche de surf classique à aileron en « D » des années 1960, un loft à toit raide fait saillie de manière symétrique à l'arrière de la structure circulaire inférieure. Face à Ka'u et South Point, l'espace loft triangulaire qui s'élève du tambour de bois et de verre est utilisé comme bureau par le propriétaire, qui peut profiter de la vue sur Point Kakio par temps clair. Inspirés des anciennes maisons hawaïennes à paroi unique, les murs et le plafond sont en bois de pin. La bibliothèque, également en pin, a été conçue par Craig Steely lui-même.

Situada cerca de Captain Cook, por encima de la bahía de Kealakekua, en la Isla Grande de Hawai, la D Fin House cuenta con ocho columnas que sostienen una estructura de vigas de madera laminada curvada y expuesta que crea un tambor de madera y vidrio revestido de acero de 17 m de diámetro. Esta estructura redonda se dobla alrededor del paisaje panorámico y sumerge al ocupante en la amplia vista de la costa de Kona. Como una clásica tabla de surf con aleta en forma de «D» de los años 60, un empinado loft con techo se proyecta simétricamente desde la parte trasera de la estructura circular inferior. Orientado hacia Ka'u y South Point, el espacio triangular del loft que se eleva desde el tambor de madera y cristal es utilizado como oficina por el propietario, que puede disfrutar de las vistas de Point Kakio en los días claros. Inspirado en las antiguas casas hawaianas de una sola pared, las paredes y el techo están hechos de madera de pino. La librería, también de pino, ha sido diseñada por el propio Craig Steely.

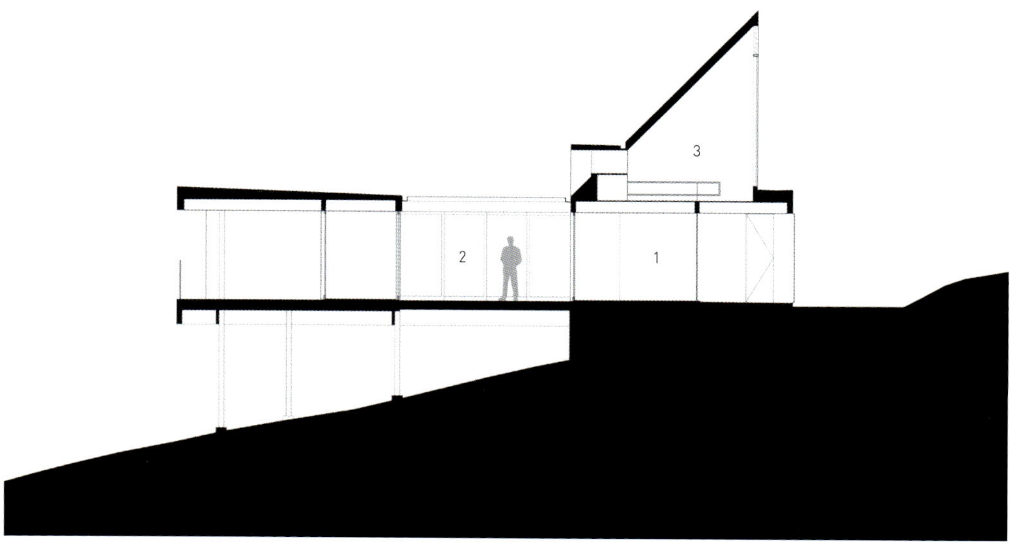

Section

1. Entry
2. Courtyard
3. Loft

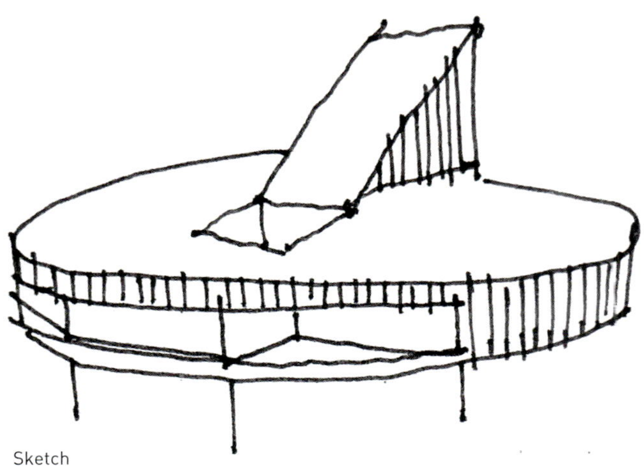

Sketch

PAM & PAUL'S

CUPERTINO, CALIFORNIA, UNITED STATES

PHOTOS © DARREN BRADLEY

Seemingly floating in the canopy of a dense oak grove in the foothills of the Santa Cruz Mountains, west of Silicon Valley, this completely glass-walled house interacts with nature without disrupting it. The open-plan living area is cantilevered into the tree canopy and features three main spaces (the living room, the office and the kitchen), each one carved out and sunk into the concrete floor to create distinct spaces. Each space is further delineated with the use of particular materials and flush mounted LED strip lighting. The sunken office sits underneath the stairs and the flooring, desk and cabinetry are all milled from a single slab of Chinese pistachio. The living room is defined by a plush purple B&B Italia "Tufty time" sofa and the kitchen/dining room features a 2 m long counter of white composite quartz.

Dieses Haus, das in einem dichten Eichenwald in den Ausläufern der Santa Cruz Mountains westlich des Silicon Valley zu schweben scheint, interagiert mit der Natur, ohne sie zu stören. Der offene Wohnbereich ist in die Baumkrone hineingekragt und besteht aus drei Haupträumen - Wohnzimmer, Büro und Küche -, die jeweils in den Betonboden eingelassen sind und so unterschiedliche Räume bilden. Jeder Raum wird durch die Verwendung besonderer Materialien und eingelassener LED-Leuchtbänder weiter abgegrenzt. Das versunkene Büro befindet sich unter der Treppe, und der Boden, der Schreibtisch und die Schränke sind aus einer einzigen Platte aus chinesischer Pistazie gefräst. Das Wohnzimmer wird von einem lilafarbenen „Tufty Time"-Sofa von B&B Italia bestimmt und die Küche/Esszimmer ist mit einer 2 m langen weißen Quarzkomposit-Arbeitsplatte ausgestattet.

Cette maison, qui semble flotter dans la canopée d'une dense forêt de chênes au pied des montagnes de Santa Cruz, à l'ouest de la Silicon Valley, interagit avec la nature sans la perturber. Le salon ouvert est en porte-à-faux dans la cime de l'arbre et comprend trois espaces principaux - le salon, le bureau et la cuisine - chacun sculpté et enfoncé dans le sol en béton pour créer des espaces distincts. Chaque espace est délimité par l'utilisation de matériaux particuliers et de bandes lumineuses LED encastrées. Le bureau en contrebas est situé sous l'escalier et le sol, le bureau et les armoires sont fabriqués à partir d'une seule plaque de pistache chinoise. Le salon est défini par un canapé violet B&B Italia « Tufty time » et la cuisine/salle à manger présente un plan de travail composite en quartz blanc de 2 m de long.

Esta casa, que parece flotar en el dosel de un denso robledal en las estribaciones de las montañas de Santa Cruz, al oeste de Silicon Valley, interactúa con la naturaleza sin perturbarla. La sala de estar, de planta abierta, está en voladizo en la copa del árbol y cuenta con tres espacios principales (la sala de estar, el despacho y la cocina), cada uno de ellos tallado y hundido en el suelo de hormigón para crear espacios distintos. Cada espacio se delimita aún más con el uso de materiales particulares y tiras de luz LED empotradas. El despacho hundido se encuentra debajo de las escaleras y el suelo, el escritorio y los armarios se han fresado a partir de una única plancha de pistacho chino. El salón está definido por un sofá púrpura de B&B Italia «Tufty time» y la cocina/comedor cuenta con una encimera de 2 m de largo de cuarzo blanco compuesto.

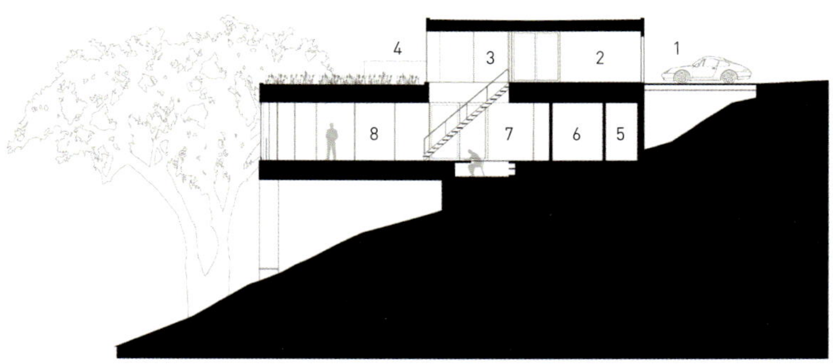

Section A-A

1. Bridge
2. Garage
3. Foyer
4. Deck
5. Mechanical
6. Laundry
7. Office
8. Living room

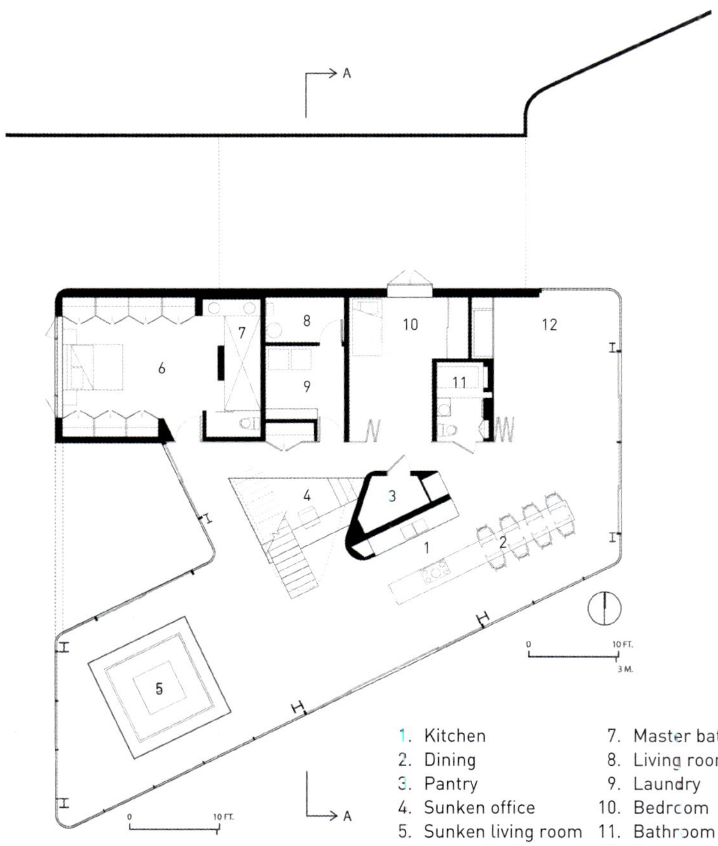

Section A-A

1. Kitchen
2. Dining
3. Pantry
4. Sunken office
5. Sunken living room
6. Master bedroom
7. Master bathroom
8. Living room
9. Laundry
10. Bedroom
11. Bathroom
12. Guest room

DE LA VEGA CANO LASSO

IGNACIO DE LA VEGA,
PILAR CANO LASSO

www.delavegacanolasso.com

Winners of the 2021 Young European Architects Award, this Madrid-based studio formed by Ignacio de la Vega and Pilar Cano Lasso specialises in bespoke sustainable projects with a focus on integrating light and surrounding nature. Known for their prefabricated Tini homes, De La Vega Cano Lasso believe that combining noble, old pieces of work found on site with other pieces prefabricated in a workshop can result in a powerful union of rich and agile architecture.

Das mit dem Young European Architects Award 2021 ausgezeichnete Madrider Büro von Ignacio de la Vega und Pilar Cano Lasso hat sich auf maßgeschneiderte, nachhaltige Projekte spezialisiert, bei denen die Integration von Licht und Natur im Mittelpunkt steht. De la Vega Cano Lasso, die für ihre Tini-Fertighäuser bekannt sind, sind davon überzeugt, dass die Kombination von edlen, gealterten Teilen, die vor Ort gefunden wurden, mit anderen, die in einer Werkstatt vorgefertigt wurden, zu einer kraftvollen Verbindung von reicher und agiler Architektur führen kann.

LA MADRIGUERA

TINI HOME OFFICE

Lauréat du prix des jeunes architectes européens 2021, ce studio madrilène formé par Ignacio de la Vega et Pilar Cano Lasso est spécialisé dans les projets durables sur mesure axés sur l'intégration de la lumière et de la nature environnante. Connu pour ses maisons préfabriquées Tini, De la Vega Cano Lasso pense que la combinaison de pièces nobles et anciennes trouvées sur place avec d'autres préfabriquées en atelier peut donner lieu à une union puissante d'architecture riche et agile.

Ganadores del Premio a los Jóvenes Arquitectos Europeos 2021, este estudio madrileño formado por Ignacio de la Vega y Pilar Cano Lasso está especializado en proyectos sostenibles a medida centrados en la integración de la luz y la naturaleza circundante. Conocidos por sus viviendas prefabricadas Tini, De la Vega Cano Lasso creen que la combinación de piezas nobles y envejecidas encontradas en el lugar con otras prefabricadas en taller puede dar como resultado una poderosa unión de arquitectura rica y ágil.

LA MADRIGUERA

MADRID, SPAIN

PHOTOS © IMAGEN SUBLIMINAL

Inspired by the privacy of cave living and their belief that modern-day's architecture has succumbed to exhibitionism, De La Vega Cano Lasso created this unusual home, breaking away from contemporary constructions. Nicknamed The Burrow for its symbolic reference to a house as a hideout, La Madriguera is made up of two structures. On the one side, the original building, a former painter's workshop, has been renovated to house a kitchen-dining area, living room and space to work from home. The loft-style interior features fixed pieces of furniture that run along the perimeter of the building, making room for a desk, kitchen work table with storage and ample seating for lounging and dining. The result is a spacious interior free from any obstacles. The other, private side hides behind a reflective construction, covered in brushed galvanised steel that reflects and diffuses the light from outside. This "introverted" space allows the user to see outside, while on the outside the garden seems to continue on the mirrored façade.

Inspiré par l'intimité de la vie dans les grottes et convaincu que l'architecture actuelle a succombé à l'exhibitionnisme, De La Vega Cano Lasso a créé cette habitation inhabituelle, en rupture avec les constructions contemporaines. Surnommée La Madriguera pour sa référence symbolique à une maison comme cachette, La Madriguera est composée de deux structures. D'une part, le bâtiment d'origine, un ancien atelier de peinture, a été réaménagé pour accueillir une cuisine-salle à manger, un salon et un espace pour travailler à domicile. L'intérieur de style loft comporte des meubles fixes qui font le tour du bâtiment, offrant de l'espace pour un bureau, une table de cuisine avec des rangements et de nombreux sièges pour se détendre et manger. Le résultat est un intérieur spacieux et épuré. L'autre côté, privé, est caché derrière une construction réfléchissante, revêtue d'acier galvanisé brossé qui reflète et diffuse la lumière de l'extérieur. Cet espace « introverti » permet une vue sur l'extérieur, tandis qu'à l'extérieur le jardin semble se prolonger dans la façade en miroir.

Inspiriert von der Intimität des Höhlenlebens und seiner Überzeugung, dass die heutige Architektur dem Exhibitionismus verfallen ist, schuf De La Vega Cano Lasso diese ungewöhnliche Behausung, die sich von den zeitgenössischen Bauten abhebt. Der Spitzname La Madriguera ist eine symbolische Anspielung auf ein Haus als Versteck und besteht aus zwei Strukturen. Einerseits wurde das ursprüngliche Gebäude, eine ehemalige Lackiererei, renoviert, um eine Küche mit Essbereich, ein Wohnzimmer und einen Raum zum Arbeiten von zu Hause aus einzurichten. Der Innenraum im Loft-Stil ist mit festen Möbeln ausgestattet, die sich um das gesamte Gebäude herum erstrecken und Platz für einen Schreibtisch, einen Küchentisch mit Stauraum und reichlich Sitzgelegenheiten zum Entspannen und Essen bieten. Das Ergebnis ist ein geräumiger und aufgeräumter Innenraum. Die andere, private Seite ist hinter einer reflektierenden Konstruktion aus gebürstetem, verzinktem Stahl verborgen, die das Licht von außen reflektiert und streut. Dieser „introvertierte" Raum gibt den Blick nach draußen frei, während sich draußen der Garten in der verspiegelten Fassade fortzusetzen scheint.

Inspirándose en la intimidad de la vida en las cuevas y en su creencia de que la arquitectura actual ha sucumbido al exhibicionismo, De La Vega Cano Lasso creó esta inusual vivienda, rompiendo con las construcciones contemporáneas. Apodada La Madriguera por su referencia simbólica a una casa como escondite, La Madriguera se compone de dos estructuras. Por un lado, el edificio original, un antiguo taller de pintura, ha sido reformado para albergar una zona de cocina-comedor, sala de estar y espacio para trabajar desde casa. El interior, de estilo loft, cuenta con muebles fijos que recorren el perímetro del edificio, dando cabida a un escritorio, una mesa de trabajo en la cocina con espacio de almacenamiento y amplios asientos para descansar y comer. El resultado es un interior espacioso y libre de obstáculos. El otro lado, el privado, se esconde tras una construcción reflectante, recubierta de acero galvanizado cepillado que refleja y difunde la luz del exterior. Este espacio «introvertido» permite ver el exterior, mientras que en el exterior el jardín parece continuar en la fachada espejada.

Axonometry

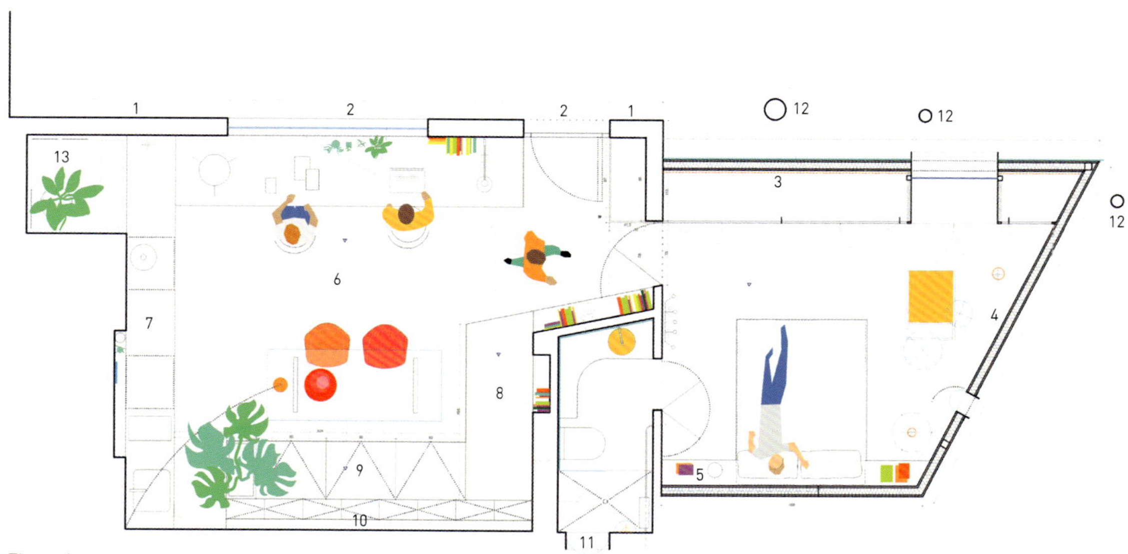

Floor plan

1. Exterior façade to be painted white
2. Exterior face of carpentry to be painted white
3. Interior finish in 1.8 cm OSB board
4. Interior finish in Galician pine planks
5. Interior finish in white painted OSB board
6. Existing MDF floor painted white
7. Birch worktop
8. Bench without backrest
9. Chest bench
10. Existing cupboards
11. New circular opening
12. Holm oak
13. Ficus robusta
14. Philodendrom

TINI HOME OFFICE

MADRID, SPAIN

PHOTOS © IMAGEN SUBLIMINAL

This prefabricated garden office was custom-built and took just 60 days to build and transport to its desired destination. Blending into the client's garden of oak trees, the Corten Steel frame module is lined with OSB Poplar wood and insulated with 12 cm of recycled cotton. The interior kitchen, cabinets and work space are made of local wood, pine and poplar, thus creating a warm and uniform interior. De La Vega Cano Lasso have maximised every inch of this 236 square-foot Tini office and created a warm and peaceful environment from which to work and observe nature.

Dieses vorgefertigte Gartenbüro wurde nach Maß gefertigt und benötigte nur 60 Tage für den Bau und den Transport an den gewünschten Bestimmungsort. Das in den Eichengarten des Kunden integrierte Corten-Stahlrahmenmodul ist mit OSB-Pappelholz verkleidet und mit 12 cm recycelter Baumwolle isoliert. Die Küche, die Schränke und der Arbeitsbereich sind aus einheimischem Holz, Kiefern- und Pappelholz, gefertigt, wodurch ein warmes und einheitliches Interieur entsteht. De La Vega Cano Lasso hat jeden Zentimeter dieses 22 m^2 großen Tini-Büros optimal genutzt und eine warme und ruhige Umgebung geschaffen, in der man arbeiten und die Natur beobachten kann.

Ce bureau de jardin préfabriqué a été construit sur mesure et il n'a fallu que 60 jours pour le construire et le transporter à la destination souhaitée. Intégré dans le jardin de chênes du client, le module de la structure en acier Corten est revêtu de bois de peuplier OSB et isolé avec 12 cm de coton recyclé. La cuisine, les armoires et l'espace de travail sont fabriqués en bois local, en pin et en peuplier, ce qui crée un intérieur chaleureux et uniforme. De La Vega Cano Lasso a tiré le meilleur parti de chaque centimètre carré de ce bureau Tini de 22 m^2 et a créé un environnement chaleureux et paisible pour travailler et observer la nature.

Esta oficina de jardín prefabricada se construyó a medida y tardó sólo 60 días en construirse y transportarse a su destino deseado. Integrado en el jardín de robles del cliente, el módulo de estructura de acero corten está revestido de madera de álamo OSB y aislado con 12 cm de algodón reciclado. La cocina interior, los armarios y el espacio de trabajo son de madera local, pino y álamo, creando así un interior cálido y uniforme. De La Vega Cano Lasso ha aprovechado al máximo cada centímetro de esta oficina Tini de 22 m^2 y ha creado un entorno cálido y tranquilo desde el que trabajar y observar la naturaleza.

DESTUDIO ARQUITECTURA

www.destudio.es

Made up of a team multidisciplinary team of professionals, Destudio Arquitectura is an architecture, design, construction and interior design studio focussed in residential, pharmacy, retail and office projects, among others. Destudio's main focus is on aesthetics and function and close attention is paid to sustainability and cost. Each design must adapt to the environment in which it will exist and adhere to high quality and precise design and innovation in new technology and materials. All interior design is marked by the studio's bespoke furniture.

Destudio Arquitectura besteht aus einem multidisziplinären Team von Fachleuten und ist ein Architektur-, Design-, Bau- und Innenarchitekturbüro, das sich unter anderem auf Wohn-, Pharma-, Einzelhandels- und Büroprojekte spezialisiert hat. Das Hauptaugenmerk von Destudio liegt auf Ästhetik und Funktion, mit einem starken Fokus auf Nachhaltigkeit und Kosten. Jeder Entwurf muss an die Umgebung, in der er entsteht, angepasst sein und hohe Qualität, präzises Design und Innovation bei neuen Technologien und Materialien aufweisen. Die gesamte Inneneinrichtung ist von maßgefertigten Möbeln geprägt.

CASA EN CHAFLÁN

Formé par une équipe pluridisciplinaire de professionnels, Destudio Arquitectura est un studio d'architecture, de conception, de construction et de décoration intérieure spécialisé dans les projets résidentiels, pharmaceutiques, commerciaux et de bureaux, entre autres. Destudio se concentre sur l'esthétique et la fonction, tout en mettant l'accent sur la durabilité et le coût. Chaque conception doit être adaptée à l'environnement dans lequel elle existera et respecter une qualité élevée, une conception de précision et l'innovation dans les nouvelles technologies et les nouveaux matériaux. L'ensemble de l'aménagement intérieur est marqué par des meubles fabriqués sur mesure.

Formado por un equipo multidisciplinar de profesionales, Destudio Arquitectura es un estudio de arquitectura, diseño, construcción e interiorismo especializado en proyectos residenciales, de farmacia, retail y oficinas, entre otros. El enfoque principal de Destudio es la estética y la función y se presta mucha atención a la sostenibilidad y al coste. Cada diseño debe adaptarse al entorno en el que va a existir y adherirse a un diseño de alta calidad y precisión y a la innovación en nuevas tecnologías y materiales. Todo el diseño interior está marcado por el mobiliario a medida.

CASA EN CHAFLÁN

VALENCIA, SPAIN

PHOTOS © MARIELA APOLLONIO

The main aim of the total renovation of this home in the centre of Valencia was to improve the living space and create a spacious home office for two people to work comfortably side by side. Re-thinking their home in the wake of the Covid pandemic, for the owners of this 1,700 square-foot apartment, it was clear the home office would be here to stay. With ample space to create a work area, Destudio decided to integrate this space into the heart of the home, with the possibility of separating it with a glass sliding door when more privacy is needed. The office also has direct access to the home's terrace. The main living-dining room is characterized by a natural oak wood-panelled curve connecting the two directions converging in this space, creating an elegant and functional room. The porcelain flooring throughout creates further continuity between the different spaces.

Hauptziel der Gesamtrenovierung dieses Hauses im Zentrum Valencias war es, den Wohnraum zu verbessern und ein geräumiges Heimbüro zu schaffen, in dem zwei Personen bequem nebeneinander arbeiten können. Nach der Covid-Pandemie überdachten die Eigentümer dieser 170 m² großen Wohnung ihr Zuhause und waren sich sicher, dass das Home-Office nicht mehr wegzudenken war. Da genügend Platz für einen Arbeitsbereich vorhanden war, entschied sich Destudio, diesen Bereich in das Herzstück des Hauses zu integrieren, mit der Möglichkeit, ihn durch eine Glasschiebetür abzutrennen, wenn mehr Privatsphäre benötigt wird. Das Büro hat auch einen direkten Zugang zur Terrasse. Das Hauptwohn- und Esszimmer zeichnet sich durch eine Kurve mit natürlicher Eichenholzvertäfelung aus, die die beiden Richtungen, die in diesem Raum zusammenlaufen, miteinander verbindet und einen eleganten und funktionalen Raum schafft. Porzellanböden im gesamten Haus schaffen eine größere Kontinuität zwischen den verschiedenen Räumen.

L'objectif principal de la rénovation totale de cette maison située dans le centre de Valence était d'améliorer l'espace de vie et de créer un bureau à domicile spacieux afin que deux personnes puissent travailler confortablement côte à côte. En repensant leur maison à la suite de la pandémie de Covid, il était clair pour les propriétaires de cet appartement de 170 m² que le bureau à domicile était là pour rester. Disposant de suffisamment d'espace pour créer une zone de travail, Destudio a décidé d'intégrer cet espace au cœur de la maison, avec la possibilité de le séparer par une porte vitrée coulissante lorsque plus d'intimité est nécessaire. Le bureau a également un accès direct à la terrasse. Le salon-salle à manger principal est caractérisé par une courbe avec des panneaux en bois de chêne naturel qui relie les deux directions qui convergent dans cet espace, créant une pièce élégante et fonctionnelle. Le sol en porcelaine dans toute la maison crée une plus grande continuité entre les différents espaces.

El objetivo principal de la reforma total de esta vivienda en el centro de Valencia era mejorar el espacio vital y crear una amplia oficina en casa para que dos personas pudieran trabajar cómodamente una al lado de la otra. Al replantearse su casa tras la pandemia de Covid, para los propietarios de este piso de 170 m² estaba claro que la oficina en casa llegaría para quedarse. Con un amplio espacio para crear una zona de trabajo, Destudio decidió integrar este espacio en el corazón de la vivienda, con la posibilidad de separarlo con una puerta corredera de cristal cuando se necesite más privacidad. El despacho también tiene acceso directo a la terraza. El salón-comedor principal se caracteriza por una curva con paneles de madera de roble natural que conecta las dos direcciones que convergen en este espacio, creando una estancia elegante y funcional. El suelo porcelánico en toda la vivienda crea una mayor continuidad entre los diferentes espacios.

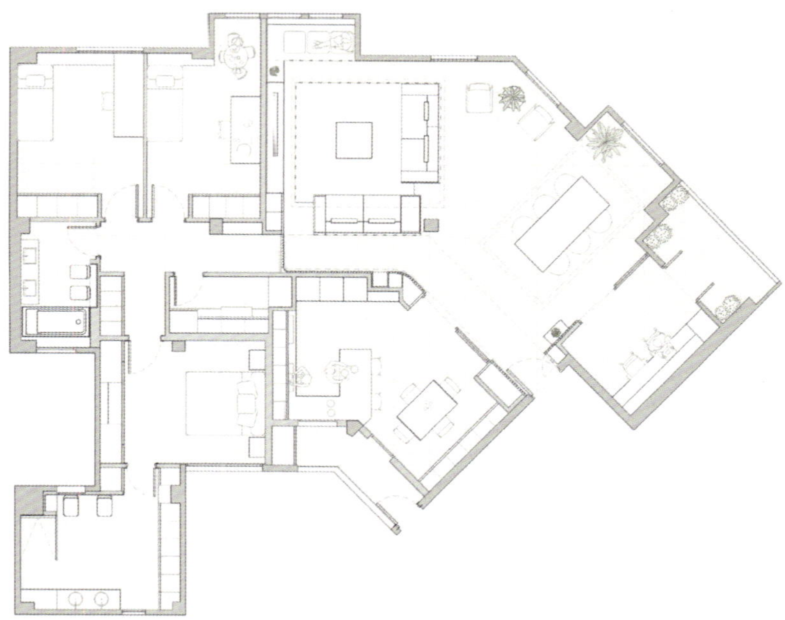

Floor plan

ESCALA ARQUITETURA

CAROLINA ESCADA,
PATRICIA LANDAU

www.escala.arq.br

After meeting at university and several years of working together, Carolina Escada and Patricia Landau created Escala Arquitetura in 2007. With complementary personalities and ideas, this Brazilian duo have acquired a harmonious design process over the years, creating unique and projects that reflect the client's identity. Escala Arquitetura focuses on residential architecture, decoration and renovation, though their work extends to commercial, hospitality and office projects.

Après s'être rencontrées à l'université et avoir travaillé ensemble pendant plusieurs années, Carolina Escada et Patricia Landau ont créé Escala Arquitetura en 2007. Avec des personnalités et des idées complémentaires, ce duo brésilien a acquis au fil des ans un processus de conception harmonieux, créant des projets uniques qui reflètent l'identité du client. Escala Arquitetura se concentre sur l'architecture, la décoration et la rénovation résidentielles, bien que son travail s'étende aux projets commerciaux, d'accueil et de bureaux.

APARTMENT RC

RR HOUSE

Nachdem sie sich an der Universität kennengelernt und mehrere Jahre zusammengearbeitet hatten, gründeten Carolina Escada und Patricia Landau im Jahr 2007 Escala Arquitetura. Mit sich ergänzenden Persönlichkeiten und Ideen hat dieses brasilianische Duo im Laufe der Jahre einen harmonischen Designprozess entwickelt, der einzigartige Projekte hervorbringt, die die Identität des Kunden widerspiegeln. Escala Arquitetura konzentriert sich auf Architektur, Dekoration und Renovierung von Wohngebäuden, arbeitet aber auch in den Bereichen Handel, Gastgewerbe und Büro.

Tras conocerse en la universidad y trabajar juntas durante varios años, Carolina Escaca y Patricia Landau crearon Escala Arquitetura en 2007. Con personalidades e ideas complementarias, este dúo brasileño ha adquirido un proceso de diseño armonioso a lo largo de los años, creando proyectos únicos y que reflejan la identidad del cliente. Escala Arquitetura se centra en la arquitectura residencial, la decoración y la renovación, aunque su trabajo se extiende a proyectos comerciales, de hostelería y de oficinas.

APARTMENT RC

RIO DE JANEIRO, BRAZIL

PHOTOS © ESCALA ARQUITETURA

The owner of this 1,076-square-foot apartment in the affluent residential neighbourhood of Jardim Botânico in Rio de Janeiro needed a space to work and a large living room to entertain. To do this, Escala Arquitetura eliminated one of the existing bedrooms and created integrated spaces. The wall separating the living room from the hallway was replaced by a central "wooden box" made with freijó leaf, a durable Brazilian wood type, featuring an office space and a multimedia stand. The smart and contemporary office space is slightly set back and is connected to one of the bedrooms by a sliding door. The office corner features a custom-built wooden desk combined with straw drawers and backlit shelves with plenty of space for books and collectibles.

Der Eigentümer dieser 325 m² großen Wohnung in der wohlhabenden Wohngegend Jardim Botânico in Rio de Janeiro benötigte einen Raum zum Arbeiten und ein großes Wohnzimmer für seine Gäste. Zu diesem Zweck hat Escala Arquitetura eines der vorhandenen Schlafzimmer entfernt und integrierte Räume geschaffen. Die Wand, die das Wohnzimmer vom Flur trennt, wurde durch eine zentrale „Holzbox" aus Freijó-Blättern, einer widerstandsfähigen brasilianischen Holzart, ersetzt, die einen Büroraum und einen Multimedia-Stand enthält. Der schlichte und moderne Büroraum ist leicht zurückgesetzt und durch eine Schiebetür mit einem der Schlafzimmer verbunden. In der Büroecke steht ein maßgefertigter Holzschreibtisch, kombiniert mit Strohschubladen und hinterleuchteten Regalen mit viel Platz für Bücher und Sammlerstücke.

Le propriétaire de cet appartement de 325 m² situé dans le quartier résidentiel aisé de Jardim Botânico à Rio de Janeiro avait besoin d'un espace pour travailler et d'un grand salon pour recevoir. Pour ce faire, Escala Arquitetura a supprimé l'une des chambres existantes et créé des espaces intégrés. Le mur séparant le salon du couloir a été remplacé par une « boîte en bois » centrale faite de feuilles de freijó, une essence de bois brésilienne très résistante, qui comprend un espace bureau et un stand multimédia. L'espace bureau contemporain et épuré est légèrement en retrait et relié à l'une des chambres par une porte coulissante. Le coin bureau comprend un bureau en bois fait sur mesure, associé à des tiroirs en paille et à des étagères rétroéclairées offrant beaucoup d'espace pour les livres et les objets de collection.

El propietario de este apartamento de 325 m² en el acomodado barrio residencial de Jardim Botânico, en Río de Janeiro, necesitaba un espacio para trabajar y un gran salón para entretenerse. Para ello, Escala Arquitetura eliminó uno de los dormitorios existentes y creó espacios integrados. La pared que separaba el salón del pasillo se sustituyó por una «caja de madera» central hecha con hoja de freijó, un tipo de madera brasileña muy resistente, que incluye un espacio de oficina y un soporte multimedia. El espacio de oficina, elegante y contemporáneo, está ligeramente replegado y conectado a uno de los dormitorios por una puerta corredera. El rincón del despacho cuenta con un escritorio de madera hecho a medida, combinado con cajones de paja y estanterías retroiluminadas con mucho espacio para libros y objetos de colección.

NACIONAL
topDRIVERS
100senna

RR HOUSE

RIO DE JANEIRO, BRAZIL

PHOTOS © ESCALA ARQUITETURA

This three-story home, winner of the CAU+Mulheres Award for interior architecture design, features a timeless interior with a mix of styles, colours and textures in each room and a different atmosphere on each floor. The owners requested integrated spaces with moments of privacy. Away from the social and daily activities going on in the rest of the house, the home office is located on the top floor. An oasis of calm, flooded with light and natural ventilation coming in through the tall windows. A large desk and open bookshelf overlook a lounge area and the rooftop terrace and pool area.

Dieses dreistöckige Haus, das mit dem CAU+Mulheres Award für Innenarchitektur ausgezeichnet wurde, zeichnet sich durch eine zeitlose Einrichtung mit einem Mix aus Stilen, Farben und Texturen in jedem Raum und einem unterschiedlichen Ambiente auf jeder Etage aus. Die Eigentümer wünschten sich integrierte Räume mit Momenten der Privatsphäre. Abseits der sozialen und alltäglichen Aktivitäten, die im restlichen Haus stattfinden, befindet sich das Home Office im obersten Stockwerk. Eine Oase der Ruhe, durchflutet von natürlichem Licht und Belüftung durch die hohen Fenster. Ein großer Schreibtisch und offene Regale führen in den Wohnbereich und auf die Dachterrasse und den Poolbereich.

Cette maison de trois étages, lauréate du prix CAU+Mulheres pour le design d'architecture intérieure, présente un intérieur intemporel avec un mélange de styles, de couleurs et de textures dans chaque pièce et une ambiance différente à chaque étage. Les propriétaires ont demandé des espaces intégrés avec des moments d'intimité. Loin des activités sociales et quotidiennes qui se déroulent dans le reste de la maison, le bureau à domicile est situé au dernier étage. Une oasis de calme, inondée de lumière naturelle et de ventilation par les hautes fenêtres. Un grand bureau et des étagères ouvertes donnent sur le salon, la terrasse sur le toit et la piscine.

Esta casa de tres plantas, ganadora del CAU+Mulheres Award de diseño de arquitectura interior, presenta un interior atemporal con una mezcla de estilos, colores y texturas en cada habitación y un ambiente diferente en cada planta. Los propietarios solicitaron espacios integrados con momentos de privacidad. Alejada de las actividades sociales y cotidianas que se desarrollan en el resto de la casa, la oficina doméstica se encuentra en la planta superior. Un oasis de calma, inundado de luz y ventilación natural que entra por las altas ventanas. Un gran escritorio y una estantería abierta dan a la zona de estar y a la terraza de la azotea y la zona de la piscina.

DON'T GROW UP
IT'S A TRAP

DON'T GROW UP
IT'S A TRAP
grimm

HUMBERT POYET

EMIL HUMBERT, CHRISTOPHE POYET

www.humbertpoyet.com

Founded in 2007, Emil Humbert and Christophe Poyet are two design and fashion enthusiasts with architecture and interior design backgrounds who have pooled their skills to provide a full range of interior design and construction services. With a focus on elegant and meticulous design, Humbert & Poyet create timeless and luxury spaces using premium materials including stone, wood and bronze. Each Humbert & Poyet design is market by their way of showcasing a space through their excellent choice of materials, lighting and decorative element.

Die 2007 gegründeten Emil Humbert und Christophe Poyet sind zwei Design- und Modebegeisterte mit Architektur- und Innenarchitektenhintergrund, die ihre Kompetenzen gebündelt haben, um ein umfassendes Angebot an Innenarchitektur- und Baudienstleistungen anzubieten. Mit ihrem Schwerpunkt auf elegantem und sorgfältigem Design schaffen Humbert & Poyet zeitlose und luxuriöse Räume unter Verwendung hochwertiger Materialien wie Stein, Holz und Bronze. Jedes Design von Humbert & Poyet zeichnet sich durch die Art und Weise aus, wie sie einen Raum durch die exzellente Auswahl von Materialien, Beleuchtung und dekorativen Elementen in Szene setzen.

BEAUMARCHAIS ROOFTOP

GRACE

Fondés en 2007, Emil Humbert et Christophe Poyet sont deux passionnés de design et de mode, issus de l'architecture et du design d'intérieur, qui ont mis en commun leurs compétences pour offrir une gamme complète de services d'aménagement intérieur et de construction. En mettant l'accent sur un design élégant et méticuleux, Humbert & Poyet créent des espaces intemporels et luxueux en utilisant des matériaux de première qualité, notamment la pierre, le bois et le bronze. Chaque design Humbert & Poyet se distingue par sa façon de mettre en valeur un espace grâce à son excellent choix de matériaux, d'éclairage et d'éléments décoratifs.

Juntos desde 2007, Emil Humbert y Christophe Poyet son dos entusiastas del diseño y la moda con formación en arquitectura y diseño de interiores que han unido sus habilidades para ofrecer una gama completa de servicios de diseño de interiores y construcción. Centrados en un diseño elegante y meticuloso, Humbert & Poyet crean espacios atemporales y lujosos utilizando materiales de primera calidad, como la piedra, la madera y el bronce. Cada diseño de Humbert & Poyet se muestra a través de su excelente elección de materiales, iluminación y elementos decorativos.

BEAUMARCHAIS ROOFTOP

PARIS, FRANCE

PHOTOS © FRANCIS AMIAND

Located on the top floor of a 1970s building with sweeping views over the French capitol's rooftops, this 91 m² apartment is marked by sliding partitions concealed in custom-made joineries designed like walls. On one side of the apartment, the walls are punctuated by bronze frames which create different spaces, such as the office and library. The office corner features bespoke storage units concealed behind the green wall and is decorated with exclusive design pieces, including a Gino Sarfatti lamp, a photograph by Bruno Staub and Christian Dior's "Ambre Nuit" candle. The "Fauteuil Direction" chair by Jean Prouvé for Vitra completes the look of this elegant home office space. The apartment matches the personality of the homeowner, a collector of contemporary art photos and vintage fixtures. Inside this apartment we can find Robert Longo's "Men in the Cities" photographs, Gino Sarfatti's "1073/3" floor lamp and the Jean Prouvé's "EM" table for Vitra.

Diese 91 m² große Wohnung befindet sich im obersten Stockwerk eines Gebäudes aus den 1970er Jahren und bietet einen atemberaubenden Blick über die Dächer der französischen Hauptstadt. Sie ist durch Schiebewände gekennzeichnet, die in maßgefertigten Tischlerarbeiten verborgen sind, die wie Wände aussehen. Auf einer Seite der Wohnung werden die Wände durch Bronzerahmen unterbrochen, die verschiedene Räume, wie das Büro und die Bibliothek, bilden. Die Büroecke ist mit maßgeschneiderten Schränken ausgestattet, die sich hinter der grünen Wand verbergen, und mit exklusiven Designerstücken dekoriert, darunter eine Lampe von Gino Sarfatti, eine Fotografie von Bruno Staub und die Kerze „Ambre Nuit" von Christian Dior. Der Stuhl „Fauteuil Direction" von Jean Prouvé für Vitra vervollständigt den Look dieses eleganten Home-Office-Bereichs. Die Wohnung entspricht der Persönlichkeit des Eigentümers, eines Sammlers von zeitgenössischen Kunstfotos und Vintage-Möbeln. In dieser Wohnung finden wir die Fotografien „Men in the Cities" von Robert Longo, die Stehleuchte „1073/3" von Gino Sarfatti und den Tisch „EM" von Jean Prouvé für Vitra.

Situé au dernier étage d'un immeuble des années 1970 offrant une vue imprenable sur les toits de la capitale française, cet appartement de 91 m² est marqué par des cloisons coulissantes dissimulées dans des menuiseries sur mesure conçues comme des murs. Sur un côté de l'appartement, les murs sont ponctués de cadres en bronze qui créent différents espaces, tels que le bureau et la bibliothèque. Le coin bureau comprend des rangements sur mesure dissimulés derrière le mur vert et est décoré de pièces de design exclusives, notamment une lampe Gino Sarfatti, une photographie de Bruno Staub et la bougie « Ambre Nuit » de Christian Dior. La chaise « Fauteuil Direction » de Jean Prouvé pour Vitra complète le look de cet élégant espace de bureau à domicile. L'appartement correspond à la personnalité du propriétaire, un collectionneur de photos d'art contemporain et de luminaires vintage. Dans cet appartement, nous pouvons trouver les photographies « Men in the Cities » de Robert Longo, le lampadaire « 1073/3 » de Gino Sarfatti et la table « EM » de Jean Prouvé pour Vitra.

Situado en la última planta de un edificio de los años 70 con amplias vistas sobre los tejados de la capital francesa, este apartamento de 91 m² está marcado por tabiques deslizantes ocultos en carpinterías hechas a medida y diseñadas como paredes. En uno de los lados del apartamento, las paredes están salpicadas de marcos de bronce que crean diferentes espacios, como el despacho y la biblioteca. El rincón del despacho cuenta con unidades de almacenamiento a medida ocultas tras la pared verde y está decorado con piezas de diseño exclusivas, como una lámpara de Gino Sarfatti, una fotografía de Bruno Staub y la vela «Ambre Nuit» de Christian Dior. La silla «Fauteuil Direction» de Jean Prouvé para Vitra completa el aspecto de este elegante espacio de oficina en casa. El apartamento está en consonancia con la personalidad del propietario, un coleccionista de fotos de arte contemporáneo y accesorios vintage. En el interior de este apartamento podemos encontrar las fotografías «Men in the Cities» de Robert Longo, la lámpara de pie «1073/3» de Gino Sarfatti y la mesa «EM» de Jean Prouvé para Vitra.

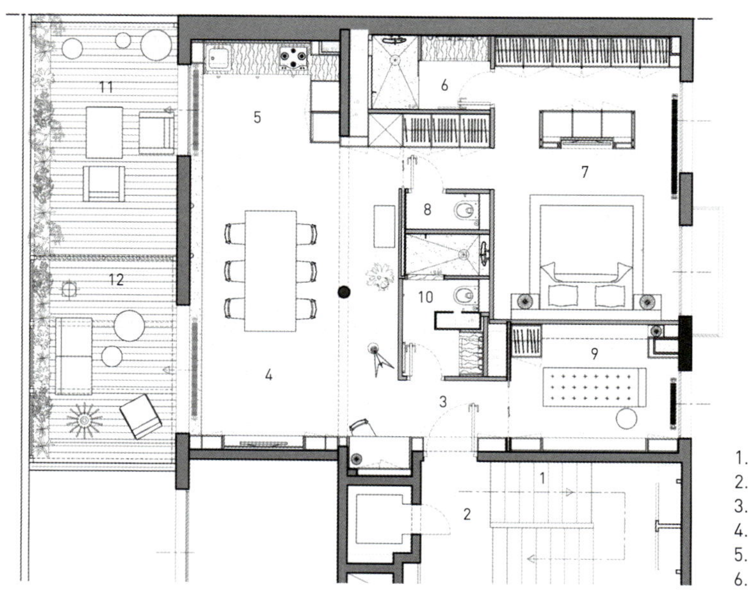

1. Stairs
2. Hall
3. Entrance
4. Living
5. Kitchen
6. Master bathroom
7. Master bedroom
8. Toilets
9. Guest bedroom
10. Guest bathroom
11. Terrace
12. Veranda

Floor plan

GRACE

MONACO CITY, MONACO

PHOTOS © FRANCIS AMIAND

Two apartments on the seafront in Monaco's exclusive Larvotto area have been transformed to create one unique space. The blend of the Riviera's French and Italian style, as well as the 1970s apartment building with its Art Deco style lobby, provide ample inspiration for the creation of a timeless interior, which exudes discreet luxury. A vintage Balancier Lightolier illuminates a Jean Prouvé desk and chair in this graceful study, which is punctuated with touches of bright colour and Paul Kowan artwork. Complementing the breath-taking exterior views over the Mediterranean, Humbert & Poyet chose the printed Palm wallpaper by Cole and Sons for the study's walls. A Gio Ponti mirror hangs above a 1950s Jean Prouvé daybed, which blends in with the palm print on the walls.

Deux appartements situés sur le front de mer dans le quartier exclusif du Larvotto à Monaco ont été transformés pour créer un espace unique. Le mélange des styles français et italien de la Riviera, ainsi que l'immeuble d'habitation des années 1970 avec son hall d'entrée de style Art déco, ont largement inspiré la création d'un intérieur intemporel, qui respire le luxe discret. Un Lightolier Balancier vintage illumine un bureau et une chaise Jean Prouvé dans ce bureau gracieux, qui est ponctué de touches de couleurs vives et d'œuvres d'art Paul Kowan. Pour compléter les vues extérieures à couper le souffle sur la Méditerranée, Humbert & Poyet a choisi le papier peint Palm imprimé de Cole and Sons pour les murs du bureau. Un miroir Gio Ponti est suspendu au-dessus d'un lit de repos Jean Prouvé des années 1950, qui se fond dans l'imprimé Palm des murs.

Zwei Wohnungen an der Strandpromenade im exklusiven Larvotto-Viertel von Monaco wurden zu einem einzigartigen Raum umgestaltet. Die Mischung aus französischem und italienischem Stil an der Riviera sowie das Apartmentgebäude aus den 1970er Jahren mit seiner Lobby im Art-déco-Stil boten reichlich Inspiration für die Gestaltung eines zeitlosen Interieurs, das diskreten Luxus ausstrahlt. Eine alte Balancier-Leuchte beleuchtet einen Jean-Prouvé-Schreibtisch und einen Jean-Prouvé-Stuhl in diesem anmutigen Arbeitszimmer, das mit leuchtenden Farbtupfern und Kunstwerken von Paul Kowan unterstrichen wird. Passend zu der atemberaubenden Aussicht auf das Mittelmeer wählten Humbert & Poyet für die Wände des Arbeitszimmers die bedruckte Tapete Palm von Cole and Sons. Ein Spiegel von Gio Ponti hängt über einem Tagesbett von Jean Prouvé aus den 1950er Jahren, das mit dem Palmenmuster an den Wänden harmoniert.

Dos apartamentos en el paseo marítimo de la exclusiva zona de Larvotto en Mónaco se han transformado para crear un espacio único. La mezcla del estilo francés e italiano de la Riviera, así como el edificio de apartamentos de los años 70, con su vestíbulo de estilo Art Decó, proporcionan una amplia inspiración para la creación de un interior atemporal, que desprende un lujo discreto. Un Balancier Lightolier vintage ilumina un escritorio y una silla de Jean Prouvé en este elegante estudio, que está salpicado de toques de color brillante y obras de arte de Paul Kowan. Como complemento a las impresionantes vistas exteriores sobre el Mediterráneo, Humbert & Poyet eligió el papel pintado Palm de Cole and Sons para las paredes del estudio. Un espejo de Gio Ponti cuelga sobre un sofá cama de Jean Prouvé de los años 50, que se combina con el estampado de palmeras de las paredes.

i29

JASPAR JANSEN, JEROEN DELLENSEN,
CHRIS COLLARIS, KODDE, G.K. VISBEEN & CO.,
SCHNEIDER INTERIEURBOUW

www.i29.nl

This award-winning Dutch interior design and architecture studio has a diverse portfolio of projects ranging from homes and hotels to offices, restaurants and other public buildings for a wide range of clients. Known for their simple, yet surprising projects, i29 partners, Jaspar Jansen, Jeroen Dellensen and Chris Collaris proudly claim they create spaces with strong identities that speak loud and clear. For each project, i29 goes back to the core and works out how to create something that inspires a better future. When working on heritage project, they embrace the opportunity to reuse qualities from the past. With new developments they focus on creating future-proof constructions. Thinking out of the box, their ultimate goal is to smart and simple with a focus on quality and efficiency.

Das preisgekrönte niederländische Büro für Innenarchitektur und Design verfügt über ein vielfältiges Portfolio an Projekten, die von Wohnhäusern und Hotels bis hin zu Büros, Restaurants und anderen öffentlichen Gebäuden für ein breites Spektrum von Kunden reichen. Die Partner von i29, Jaspar Jansen, Jeroen Dellensen und Chris Collaris, sind bekannt für ihre schlichten und doch auffälligen Projekte und sind stolz darauf, Räume mit einer starken Identität zu schaffen, die laut und deutlich spricht. Bei jedem Projekt besinnt sich i29 auf das Wesentliche und arbeitet daran, etwas zu schaffen, das eine bessere Zukunft inspiriert. Bei der Arbeit an historischen Projekten nutzen sie die Gelegenheit, Qualitäten aus der Vergangenheit wiederzuverwenden. Bei neuen Projekten konzentrieren sie sich auf die Schaffung zukunftsfähiger Gebäude. Ihr oberstes Ziel ist es, intelligent und einfach zu sein und sich auf Qualität und Effizienz zu konzentrieren.

CANAL HOUSE

Ce cabinet néerlandais d'architecture et de design d'intérieur primé possède un portefeuille de projets diversifiés, allant de maisons et d'hôtels à des bureaux, des restaurants et d'autres bâtiments publics pour un large éventail de clients. Connus pour leurs projets simples mais frappants, les partenaires d'i29, Jaspar Jansen, Jeroen Dellensen et Chris Collaris, revendiquent fièrement la création d'espaces aux identités fortes qui parlent haut et fort. Pour chaque projet, i29 retourne à l'essentiel et s'efforce de créer quelque chose qui inspire un avenir meilleur. Lorsqu'ils travaillent sur des projets patrimoniaux, ils profitent de l'occasion pour réutiliser les qualités du passé. Pour les nouveaux projets, ils s'attachent à créer des bâtiments à l'épreuve du temps. Leur objectif ultime est d'être intelligent et simple, en se concentrant sur la qualité et l'efficacité.

Este galardonado estudio holandés de diseño de interiores y arquitectura cuenta con una variada cartera de proyectos que van desde viviendas y hoteles hasta oficinas, restaurantes y otros edificios públicos para una amplia gama de clientes. Conocidos por sus proyectos sencillos pero sorprendentes, los socios de i29, Jaspar Jansen, Jeroen Dellensen y Chris Collaris, afirman con orgullo que crean espacios con identidades fuertes que hablan alto y claro. Para cada proyecto, i29 se remonta a la esencia y trabaja para crear algo que inspire un futuro mejor. Cuando trabajan en proyectos de patrimonio, aprovechan la oportunidad de reutilizar cualidades del pasado. En el caso de los nuevos proyectos, se centran en crear construcciones preparadas para el futuro. Su objetivo final es ser inteligentes y sencillos, centrándose en la calidad y la eficiencia.

CANAL HOUSE

AMSTERDAM, THE NETHERLANDS

PHOTOS © EWOUT HUIBERS

This severely neglected, late 17th century canal house in Amsterdam was completely renovated and turned into a bright and colourful new family home. Together with a team of specialists, award-winning architects i29 created a bright white interior with bursts of colour throughout defining specific living spaces. Grey-stained walls and stairs connect the ground-floor kitchen, the heart of this family home, to the upstairs study room and first-floor living area. The grey colour continues into the study area until it is broken up by a colourful intervention of sage green to define the purpose of this space: work. Behind the green desk is a built-in grey shelving unit with a window on the lower shelf, which visually connects the downstairs kitchen.

Dieses stark vernachlässigte Kanalhaus aus dem späten 17. Jahrhundert wurde vollständig renoviert und in ein helles und farbenfrohes neues Familienhaus verwandelt. Gemeinsam mit einem Team von Spezialisten haben die preisgekrönten Architekten von i29 ein helles, weißes Interieur mit farbigen Akzenten geschaffen, die bestimmte Wohnbereiche definieren. Graue Wände und eine Treppe verbinden die Küche im Erdgeschoss, das Herzstück dieses Familienhauses, mit dem Arbeitszimmer im Obergeschoss und dem Wohnzimmer im ersten Stock. Die graue Farbe setzt sich im Arbeitsbereich fort, bis sie durch eine farbige Intervention in Salbeigrün durchbrochen wird, um den Zweck dieses Raums zu definieren: Arbeit. Hinter dem grünen Schreibtisch befindet sich ein graues Bücherregal mit einem Fenster im unteren Regal, das eine visuelle Verbindung zur Küche im Erdgeschoss herstellt.

Cette maison du canal de la fin du XVIIe siècle, très négligée, a été entièrement rénovée et transformée en une nouvelle maison familiale lumineuse et colorée. En collaboration avec une équipe de spécialistes, les architectes primés i29 ont créé un intérieur d'un blanc éclatant avec des touches de couleur définissant des espaces de vie spécifiques. Des murs et des escaliers de teinte grise relient la cuisine du rez-de-chaussée, le cœur de cette maison familiale, à la salle d'étude de l'étage et au salon du premier étage. La couleur grise se poursuit dans la zone d'étude jusqu'à ce qu'elle soit interrompue par une intervention colorée en vert sauge pour définir l'objectif de cet espace : le travail. Derrière le bureau vert se trouve une bibliothèque grise encastrée avec une fenêtre sur l'étagère du bas, qui établit un lien visuel avec la cuisine du rez-de-chaussée.

Esta casa del canal de finales del siglo XVII, muy descuidada, se renovó por completo y se convirtió en una nueva casa familiar brillante y colorida. Junto con un equipo de especialistas, los galardonados arquitectos i29 crearon un interior blanco y luminoso con estallidos de color que definen los espacios habitables específicos. Las paredes y las escaleras teñidas de gris conectan la cocina de la planta baja, el corazón de esta casa familiar, con la sala de estudio de la planta superior y el salón de la primera planta. El color gris continúa en la zona de estudio hasta que se rompe con una colorida intervención de verde salvia para definir la finalidad de este espacio: el trabajo. Detrás del escritorio verde hay una estantería gris empotrada con una ventana en el estante inferior, que conecta visualmente con la cocina de la planta baja.

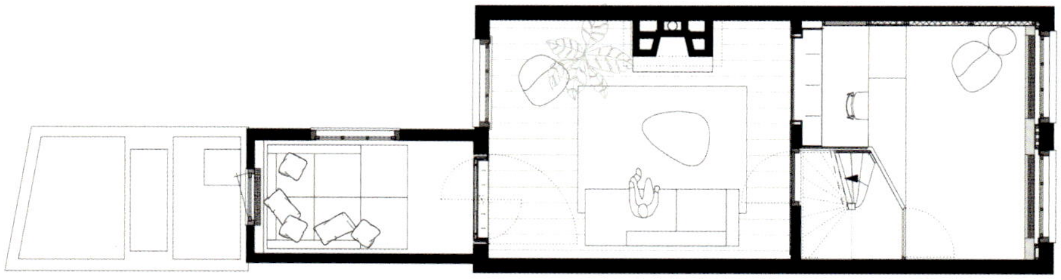

First floor plan

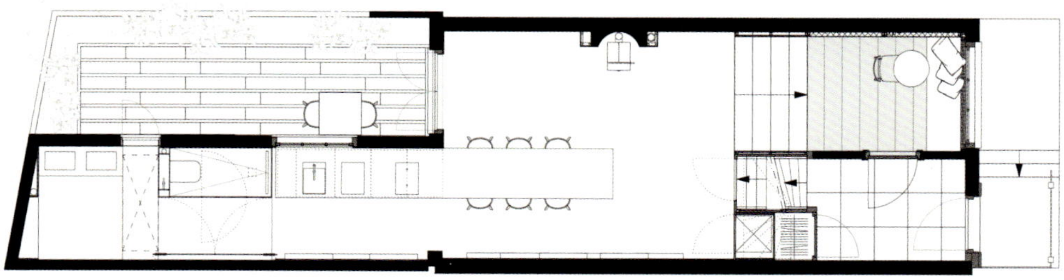

Ground floor plan

turn
the
page

3D section

IDIN ARCHITECTS

JERAVEJ HONGSAKUL, SARALEE SITTIGAROON, SUPACHAI PHIROMRACH, SAKORN THONGDOANG, THUWANONT RUANGKANOKSILP, WITH PAKANUT SIRIPRASOPSOTHORN (STRUCTURAL ENGINEER) AND EAKACHAI HAMHOMVONG, PANOT KUAKOOLWONG (SYSTEM ENGINEERS)

www.idin-architects.com

Founded in 2004, IDIN is an acronym for Integrating Design Into Nature and describes how IDIN Architects perceive nature as the ecology around us and how we can merge architecture with nature in different ways. The word "idin" is also a Thai word used to describe the scent released by the soil after rainfall, which perfectly implies the tropical climate of Thailand. IDIN's design philosophy centres on both the aesthetic and the practical, taking into account the different needs and requirements of each project and placing special importance on the environment.

Das 2004 gegründete Unternehmen IDIN steht für Integrating Design Into Nature und beschreibt, wie seine Architekten die Natur als die uns umgebende Ökologie wahrnehmen und wie wir Architektur und Natur auf unterschiedliche Weise miteinander verbinden können. Das Wort „idin" ist auch ein thailändisches Wort, das den Duft beschreibt, den der Boden nach dem Regen verströmt, was das tropische Klima Thailands perfekt widerspiegelt. Die Designphilosophie von IDIN konzentriert sich sowohl auf Ästhetik als auch auf Zweckmäßigkeit, wobei die unterschiedlichen Bedürfnisse und Anforderungen eines jeden Projekts berücksichtigt werden und der Umwelt besondere Bedeutung beigemessen wird.

JB HOUSE

Fondée en 2004, IDIN est l'acronyme de Integrating Design Into Nature et décrit la façon dont ses architectes perçoivent la nature comme l'écologie qui nous entoure et comment nous pouvons fusionner l'architecture avec la nature de différentes manières. Le mot « idin » est également un mot thaïlandais qui est utilisé pour décrire l'odeur dégagée par le sol après les pluies, ce qui implique parfaitement le climat tropical de la Thaïlande. La philosophie de conception d'IDIN se concentre à la fois sur l'esthétique et la praticité, en tenant compte des différents besoins et exigences de chaque projet et en accordant une importance particulière à l'environnement.

Fundada en 2004, DIN es un acrónimo de Integrating Design Into Nature (integración del diseño en la naturaleza) y describe cómo sus arquitectos perciben la naturaleza como la ecología que nos rodea y cómo podemos fusionar la arquitectura con la naturaleza de diferentes maneras. La palabra «idin» es también una palabra tailandesa que se utiliza para describir el aroma que desprende el suelo después de las lluvias, lo que implica perfectamente el clima tropical de Tailandia. La filosofía de diseño de IDIN se centra tanto en lo estético como en lo práctico, teniendo en cuenta las diferentes necesidades y requisitos de cada proyecto y dando especial importancia al medio ambiente.

JB HOUSE

NAKHON PATHOM, THAILAND

PHOTOS © KETSIREE WONGWAN

JB House is a truly unique home, which reflects the lifestyle of two people with different routines and activities. It is designed in such a way that allows each user to carry out their activities separately and simultaneously. The users' two main activities, publishing and cooking, are spread over two floors. The woman, a book lover with a passion for drawing, whose main activity is in the publishing field, takes the upper level, where a large sheet of glass serves as her working table. This transparent table creates a visual connection to the kitchen island on the lower floor, where the man, a photography lover and baker, carries out his main activity which revolves around the kitchen island. By stacking the spaces of the kitchen island and the working table at the same location, IDIN Architects create an interlocking element that ties the whole house together. The upper level has three connecting steps with a glass window, which serve as additional visual connections between the two users. The upper level is also covered with double wood screens, which can be opened or closed for privacy and heat protection.

JB House ist ein wirklich einzigartiges Haus, das den Lebensstil von zwei Menschen mit unterschiedlichen Routinen und Aktivitäten widerspiegelt. Es ist so konzipiert, dass jeder Benutzer seine Tätigkeiten getrennt und gleichzeitig ausführen kann. Die beiden Haupttätigkeiten der Bewohner, das Verlegen und das Kochen, sind auf zwei Etagen verteilt. Die Frau, eine Bücher- und Zeichenliebhaberin, deren Haupttätigkeit das Verlegen ist, bewohnt das obere Stockwerk, wo eine große Glasplatte als Arbeitstisch dient. Dieser transparente Tisch schafft eine visuelle Verbindung mit der Kücheninsel im unteren Stockwerk, wo der Mann, ein Fotoliebhaber und Bäcker, seiner Haupttätigkeit nachgeht. Durch die Anordnung der Kücheninsel und des Arbeitstisches am selben Ort schaffen die IDIN-Architekten ein verbindendes Element, das das ganze Haus zusammenhält. Die obere Ebene verfügt über drei Verbindungsstufen mit einem Glasfenster, die als zusätzliche Sichtverbindung zwischen den beiden Nutzern dienen. Das obere Stockwerk ist ebenfalls mit doppelten Holzschirmen bedeckt, die geöffnet oder geschlossen werden können, um Privatsphäre und Wärme zu schützen.

JB House est une maison vraiment unique, qui reflète le style de vie de deux personnes ayant des routines et des activités différentes. Il est conçu de telle manière qu'il permet à chaque utilisateur de mener ses activités séparément et simultanément. Les deux principales activités des habitants, l'édition et la cuisine, sont réparties sur deux étages. La femme, amoureuse des livres et du dessin, dont l'activité principale est l'édition, occupe le niveau supérieur, où une grande plaque de verre lui sert de table de travail. Cette table transparente crée un lien visuel avec l'îlot de cuisine situé au niveau inférieur, où l'homme, amateur de photographie et boulanger, exerce son activité principale. En superposant les espaces de l'îlot de cuisine et de la table de travail au même endroit, les architectes d'IDIN créent un élément de liaison qui relie l'ensemble de la maison. Le niveau supérieur comporte trois marches de liaison avec une fenêtre en verre, qui servent de connexions visuelles supplémentaires entre les deux utilisateurs. Le niveau supérieur est également couvert de doubles écrans en bois, qui peuvent être ouverts ou fermés pour préserver l'intimité et la chaleur.

JB House es una vivienda realmente única, que refleja el estilo de vida de dos personas con rutinas y actividades diferentes. Está diseñada de tal manera que permite a cada usuario realizar sus actividades por separado y simultáneamente. Las dos actividades principales de los habitantes , publicar y cocinar, se reparten en dos plantas. La mujer, amante de los libros y apasionada del dibujo, cuya actividad principal es la edición, ocupa el nivel superior, donde una gran lámina de cristal le sirve de mesa de trabajo. Esta mesa transparente crea una conexión visual con la isla de cocina de la planta inferior, donde el hombre, amante de la fotografía y panadero, desarrolla su actividad principal. Al apilar los espacios de la isla de cocina y la mesa de trabajo en el mismo lugar, los arquitectos de IDIN crean un elemento de unión que vincula toda la casa. El nivel superior tiene tres escalones de conexión con una ventana de cristal, que sirven como conexiones visuales adicionales entre los dos usuarios. El nivel superior también está cubierto con pantallas dobles de madera, que pueden abrirse o cerrarse para proteger la intimidad y el calor.

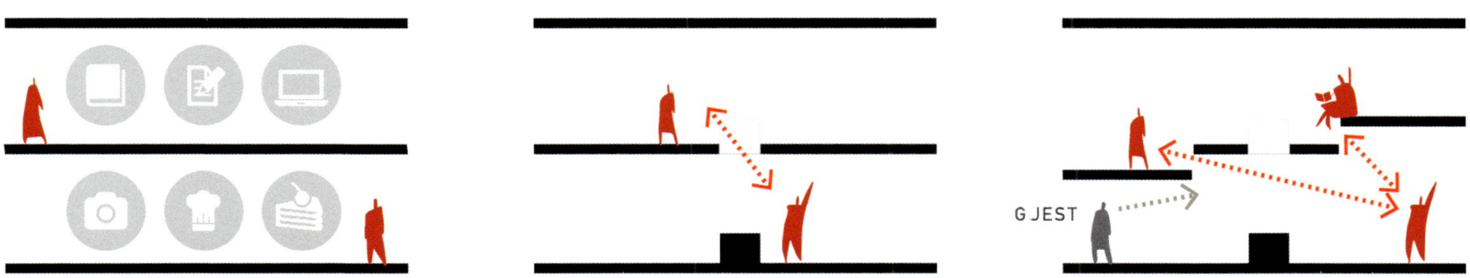

Concept diagrams

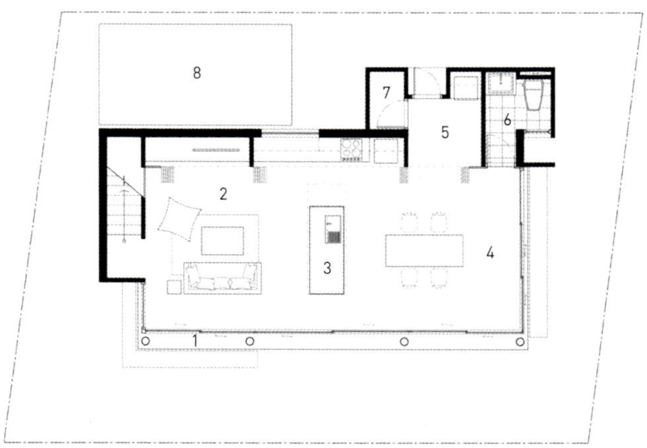

First floor plan

1. Entrance
2. Living area
3. Kitchen island
4. Dining area
5. Laundry
6. Bathroom
7. Storage
8. Parking

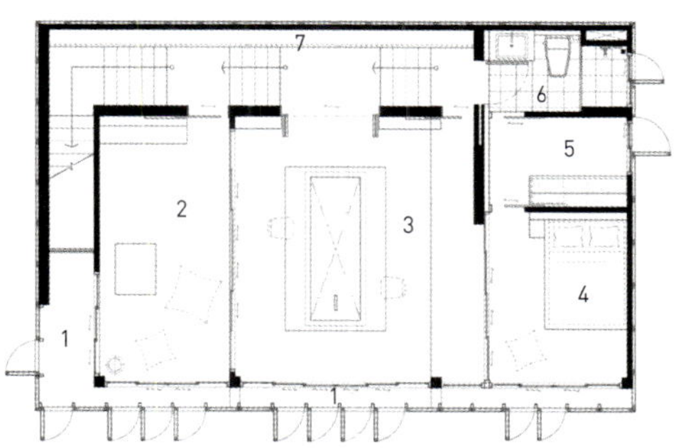

First floor plan

1. Balcony
2. Bedroom
3. Working room
4. Master bedrooom
5. Walk-in closet
6. Bathroom
7. Bookshelves

IKER LÓPEZ ESTUDIO

IKER LÓPEZ

www.ikerlopez.com

After several years with the Mórula collective, Iker López founded his studio in 2013. With offices in Madrid and Bilbao, Iker López Estudio develop a wide range of architecture and refurbishment projects throughout the Spanish territory. All of Iker López Estudio's projects start with observing and finding something in the existing work that can be a tool for new strategies of work and research and exploring all possibilities of design. Iker López also collaborates with other studios, including Empty, Izaskun Chinchilla and IDOM/ACXT and is a professor of graphic expression at the polytechnic school of Antonio de Nebrija University.

Nach mehreren Jahren im Kollektiv Mórula gründete Iker López 2013 sein Studio. Mit Büros in Madrid und Bilbao entwickelt Iker López Estudio eine breite Palette von Architektur- und Sanierungsprojekten im gesamten spanischen Raum. Alle Projekte von Iker López Estudio beginnen mit der Beobachtung und der Suche nach etwas in der bestehenden Arbeit, das als Werkzeug für neue Arbeits- und Forschungsstrategien und die Erkundung aller Möglichkeiten des Designs dienen kann. Iker López arbeitet auch mit anderen Studios zusammen, darunter Empty, Izaskun Chinchilla und IDOM/ACXT, und ist Professor für grafischen Ausdruck an der Polytechnischen Schule der Universität Antonio de Nebrija.

ESTRELLA RENOVATION

Après plusieurs années au sein du collectif Mórula, Iker López a fondé son studio en 2013. Avec des bureaux à Madrid et Bilbao, Iker López Estudio développe un large éventail de projets d'architecture et de rénovation sur l'ensemble du territoire espagnol. Tous les projets d'Iker López Estudio commencent par observer et trouver quelque chose dans l'œuvre existante qui peut être un outil pour de nouvelles stratégies de travail et de recherche et explorer toutes les possibilités de conception. Iker López collabore également avec d'autres studios, notamment Empty, Izaskun Chinchilla et IDOM/ACXT et est professeur d'expression graphique à l'école polytechnique de l'université Antonio de Nebrija.

Tras varios años en el colectivo Mórula, Iker López fundó su estudio en 2013. Con oficinas en Madrid y Bilbao, Iker López Estudio desarrolla un amplio abanico de proyectos de arquitectura y rehabilitación en todo el territorio español. Todos los proyectos de Iker López Estudio parten de observar y encontrar algo en la obra existente que pueda ser una herramienta para nuevas estrategias de trabajo e investigación y explorar todas las posibilidades del diseño. Iker López también colabora con otros estudios, como Empty, Izaskun Chinchilla e IDOM/ACXT y es profesor de expresión gráfica en la escuela politécnica de la Universidad Antonio de Nebrija.

ESTRELLA RENOVATION

MADRID, SPAIN

PHOTOS © IKER LOPEZ STUDIO

This 160 m² apartment in the residential neighbourhood of Estrella, Madrid, has been turned into a chameleon-like home for a father of four. A home which adapts and takes on two completely different forms of living every two weeks; catering to the lifestyle of a single, cosmopolitan man on the one hand and that of a family man with four children that co-habit the space twice a month. Taking inspiration from the homeowner's passion for aviation and books, Iker López came up with the idea of a bookcase as a central structure, which conceptually separates the dwelling into two distinct, yet connected areas. Situated in what used to be a dark entrance hall, this space now feels light and airy and serves as a border between the home's different functions. Surrounded by the children's bedrooms, the central structure serves as a bookcase and workspace for the four children. The work surface is created from laser-cut steel sheets and the shelves are made of white micro-perforated sheet metal to allow for maximum transparency. Vertical rods connect the shelves and support the weight of all the books.

Diese 160 m² große Wohnung im Madrider Wohnviertel Estrella wurde in ein chamäleonartiges Zuhause für einen vierfachen Vater verwandelt. Eine Wohnung, die sich anpasst und alle zwei Wochen zwei völlig unterschiedliche Wohnformen annimmt: einerseits den Lebensstil eines alleinstehenden, kosmopolitischen Mannes und andererseits den eines Familienvaters mit vier Kindern, der zweimal im Monat in der Wohnung wohnt. Inspiriert von der Leidenschaft des Hausbesitzers für die Luftfahrt und für Bücher kam Iker López auf die Idee eines Bücherschranks als zentrale Struktur, die die Wohnung konzeptionell in zwei unterschiedliche, aber miteinander verbundene Bereiche trennt. Dieser Raum, der sich in einer ehemals dunklen Eingangshalle befand, wirkt nun hell und luftig und dient als Grenze zwischen den verschiedenen Funktionen des Hauses. Die zentrale Struktur, die von den Kinderzimmern umgeben ist, dient als Bücherregal und Arbeitsbereich für die vier Kinder. Die Arbeitsfläche besteht aus lasergeschnittenen Stahlblechen, und die Regale sind aus weißem, mikroperforiertem Blech gefertigt, um eine maximale Transparenz zu gewährleisten. Vertikale Stangen verbinden die Regale und tragen das Gewicht aller Bücher.

Cet appartement de 160 m² situé dans le quartier résidentiel d'Estrella, à Madrid, a été transformé en une maison caméléon pour un père de quatre enfants. Une maison qui s'adapte et adopte deux formes de vie complètement différentes toutes les deux semaines ; répondant au style de vie d'un homme célibataire et cosmopolite d'une part et à celui d'un père de famille avec quatre enfants qui cohabitent dans l'espace deux fois par mois. S'inspirant de la passion du propriétaire pour l'aviation et les livres, Iker López a eu l'idée d'une bibliothèque comme structure centrale, qui sépare conceptuellement le logement en deux zones distinctes, mais reliées. Situé dans ce qui était auparavant un hall d'entrée sombre, cet espace est désormais léger et aéré et sert de frontière entre les différentes fonctions de la maison. Entourée par les chambres des enfants, la structure centrale sert de bibliothèque et d'espace de travail pour les quatre enfants. Le plan de travail est créé à partir de tôles d'acier découpées au laser et les étagères sont réalisées en tôle microperforée blanche pour permettre une transparence maximale. Des tiges verticales relient les étagères et supportent le poids de tous les livres.

Este apartamento de 160 m² en el barrio residencial de Estrella, Madrid, se ha convertido en un hogar camaleónico para un padre de cuatro hijos. Una vivienda que se adapta y adopta dos formas de vida completamente diferentes cada dos semanas; atendiendo al estilo de vida de un hombre soltero y cosmopolita por un lado y al de un padre de familia con cuatro hijos que cohabitan el espacio dos veces al mes. Inspirándose en la pasión del propietario por la aviación y los libros, a Iker López se le ocurrió la idea de una librería como estructura central, que separa conceptualmente la vivienda en dos zonas distintas, pero conectadas. Situada en lo que antes era un oscuro vestíbulo de entrada, este espacio ahora se siente ligero y aireado y sirve de frontera entre las diferentes funciones de la casa. Rodeada por los dormitorios de los niños, la estructura central sirve de librería y espacio de trabajo para los cuatro niños. La superficie de trabajo se ha creado a partir de láminas de acero cortadas con láser y los estantes son de chapa blanca microperforada para permitir la máxima transparencia. Las barras verticales conectan los estantes y soportan el peso de todos los libros.

Premio Nacional del Comic 2008
LA NOVELA GRÁFICA EN LA QUE SE BASA LA PELÍCULA

1001 PELÍCULAS
JOHN FORD
CINE DE LOS 70
STANLEY KUBRICK
Kubrick
MICHEL CIMENT
THE STANLEY KUBRICK ARCHIVES
THE PEDRO ALMODÓVAR ARCHIVES
RICHARD AVEDON PORTRAITS

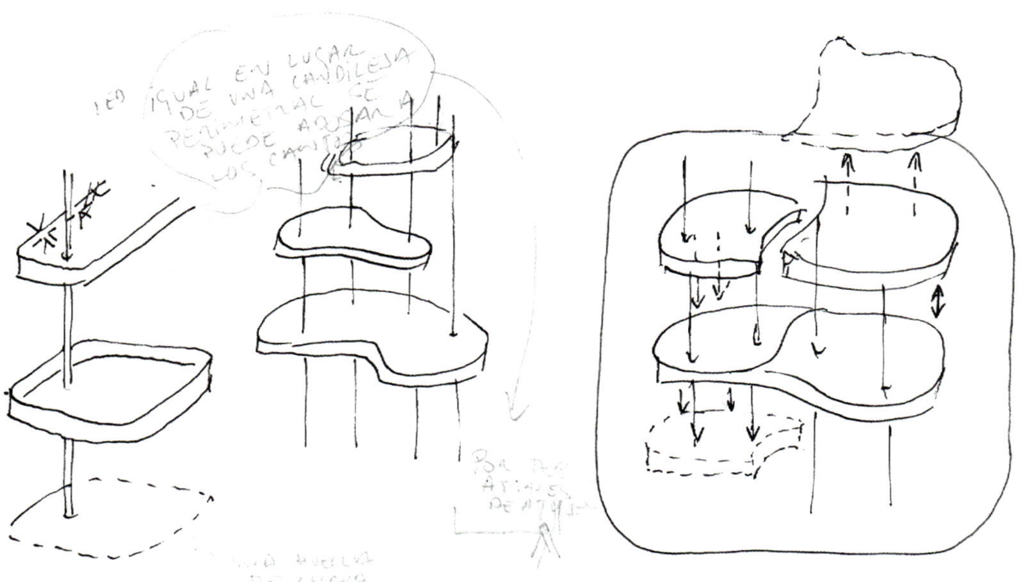

Sketch

ROBERT CAPA
MAGNUM
RICHARD ESTES
La Chapelle Land

JACOB LAWS INTERIOR DESIGN

JACOB LAWS

www.jacoblaws.com

St Louis-born Jacob Laws launched his own design firm, Jacob Laws Interior Design in 2015, with a historic headquarter office in Charleston, South Carolina, added in Spring 2022. Focused on creating aesthetically beautiful, innovative and functional living spaces, Jacob Laws adds his personal style to each project to create sophisticated and dynamic interiors. His work ranges from luxury condominiums, urban loft redesigns and family retreats to broad-spectrum planning and implementation for new developments. Taking inspiration from art, travel, fashion, culture and history, Jacob Laws likes to play with the mix of old and new, and traditional and modern. Creative without being directed by a formula is Jacob Laws' motto for contemporary interiors that transcend trends and tell the story of the clients.

Der in St. Louis geborene Jacob Laws gründete 2015 sein eigenes Designbüro, Jacob Laws Interior Design, das im Frühjahr 2022 um ein historisches Hauptbüro in Charleston, South Carolina, erweitert wurde. Jacob Laws konzentriert sich auf die Gestaltung ästhetisch schöner, innovativer und funktionaler Lebensräume und verleiht jedem Projekt seinen persönlichen Stil, um anspruchsvolle und dynamische Innenräume zu schaffen. Seine Arbeit reicht von luxuriösen Eigentumswohnungen, der Neugestaltung städtischer Lofts und Familienresidenzen bis hin zur umfassenden Planung und Umsetzung von Neubauprojekten. Jacob Laws lässt sich von Kunst, Reisen, Mode, Kultur und Geschichte inspirieren und spielt gerne mit der Mischung aus Alt und Neu, Tradition und Moderne. Kreativ sein, ohne sich von einer Formel leiten zu lassen - das ist Jacob Laws' Motto für zeitgemäße Inneneinrichtungen, die über Trends hinausgehen und die Geschichte der Kunden erzählen.

TOWN & COUNTRY

HORTENSE PLACE

PRICE ROAD

Originaire de Saint-Louis, Jacob Laws a lancé sa propre entreprise de design, Jacob Laws Interior Design, en 2015, avec un siège social historique à Charleston, en Caroline du Sud, ajouté au printemps 2022. Axé sur la création d'espaces de vie esthétiquement beaux, innovants et fonctionnels, Jacob Laws ajoute son style personnel à chaque projet pour créer des intérieurs sophistiqués et dynamiques. Son travail s'étend des condominiums de luxe, des réaménagements de lofts urbains et des retraites familiales à la planification et à la mise en œuvre à large spectre de nouveaux développements. S'inspirant de l'art, des voyages, de la mode, de la culture et de l'histoire, Jacob Laws aime jouer avec le mélange de l'ancien et du nouveau, du traditionnel et du moderne. Créer sans être guidé par une formule, telle est la devise de Jacob Laws pour des intérieurs contemporains qui transcendent les tendances et racontent l'histoire des clients.

Jacob Laws, nacido en San Luis, puso en marcha su propia empresa de diseño, Jacob Laws Interior Design, en 2015, y en la primavera de 2022 añadió una sede histórica en Charleston, Carolina del Sur. Centrado en la creación de espacios de vida estéticamente bellos, innovadores y funcionales, Jacob Laws añade su estilo personal a cada proyecto para crear interiores sofisticados y dinámicos. Su trabajo abarca desde condominios de lujo, re diseños de lofts urbanos y retiros familiares hasta la planificación e implementación de amplio espectro para nuevos desarrollos. Inspirándose en el arte, los viajes, la moda, la cultura y la historia, a Jacob Laws le gusta jugar con la mezcla de lo antiguo y lo nuevo, y lo tradicional y lo moderno. Ser creativo sin guiarse por una fórmula es el lema de Jacob Laws para conseguir interiores contemporáneos que trasciendan las tendencias y cuenten la historia de los clientes.

TOWN & COUNTRY

ST. LOUIS, MISSOURI, UNITED STATES

PHOTOS © ALISE O'BRIEN

Looking for an elegant, masculine interior design to reflect the owner's personality in this study, Jacob Laws chose sleek, uncomplicated pieces that could complement each other. The cantilevered, floating white shelves, which lend a gallery-like vibe, sit above a minimalist linear white cabinet, complement the composition of natural materials and 1970s linear seating. A brass-framed floating sofa upholstered in a rust velvet situated on one side of the room contrasts with the dark, moody walls, and gives a distinct masculine touch. On the other side of the room, a sleek natural wood desk perfectly combines with the Eames plywood chair and Eames Executive desk chair in Slate pebbled leather.

À la recherche d'une décoration intérieure élégante et masculine pour refléter la personnalité du propriétaire de ce bureau, Jacob Laws a choisi des pièces épurées et simples qui pouvaient se compléter. Les étagères blanches flottantes en porte-à-faux, qui donnent une impression de galerie, se trouvent au-dessus d'une armoire blanche linéaire minimaliste, et complètent la composition de matériaux naturels et de sièges linéaires des années 1970. Un canapé flottant à cadre en laiton, tapissé d'un velours rouille, situé sur un côté de la pièce, contraste avec les murs sombres et sombres, et donne une touche masculine distincte. De l'autre côté de la pièce, un bureau épuré en bois naturel s'associe parfaitement à la chaise Eames en contreplaqué et au fauteuil de bureau Eames Executive en cuir galet ardoise.

Auf der Suche nach einer eleganten, maskulinen Inneneinrichtung, die die Persönlichkeit des Eigentümers in diesem Arbeitszimmer widerspiegeln sollte, wählte Jacob Laws schlichte, unkomplizierte Stücke, die sich gegenseitig ergänzen konnten. Die freitragenden, schwebenden weißen Regale, die eine galerieähnliche Atmosphäre vermitteln, sitzen über einem minimalistischen, geradlinigen weißen Schrank und ergänzen die Komposition aus natürlichen Materialien und geradlinigen Sitzmöbeln aus den 1970er Jahren. Ein mit rostfarbenem Samt bezogenes, schwebendes Sofa mit Messingrahmen auf der einen Seite des Raumes kontrastiert mit den dunklen, stimmungsvollen Wänden und verleiht einen deutlich maskulinen Touch. Auf der anderen Seite des Raumes steht ein schlichter Schreibtisch aus Naturholz, der perfekt mit dem Eames-Sperrholzstuhl und dem Eames Executive-Schreibtischstuhl aus schieferfarbenem Kiesel-Leder kombiniert ist.

Buscando un diseño interior elegante y masculino que reflejara la personalidad del propietario de este estudio, Jacob Laws eligió piezas elegantes y sin complicaciones que pudieran complementarse entre sí. Las estanterías blancas flotantes en voladizo, que dan un aire de galería, se sitúan encima de un armario blanco lineal minimalista y complementan la composición de materiales naturales y los asientos lineales de los años 70. Un sofá flotante con marco de latón y tapizado en terciopelo oxidado, situado en un lado de la sala, contrasta con las paredes oscuras y malhumoradas, y aporta un marcado toque masculino. En el otro lado de la sala, un elegante escritorio de madera natural combina a la perfección con la silla de madera contrachapada Eames y el sillón de escritorio Eames Executive de cuero granulado Slate.

HORTENSE PLACE

ST. LOUIS, MISSOURI, UNITED STATES

PHOTOS © ALISE O'BRIEN

This teenage-girl-bedroom-turned-retiree-study is a real masculine metamorphosis. As with all of his projects, Jacob Laws tried to tell his client's story using design as his medium and with a unique result. A range of periods and international styles sit together comfortably in this informal, worldly and sophisticated space. Men's wool suiting fabric is turned into wall covering, complemented by custom blackened steel and wood open etagere towers found at a San Francisco Designer Showhouse.

Dieses Schlafzimmer eines Teenagers, das sich in ein Arbeitszimmer für Rentner verwandelt hat, ist eine echte männliche Metamorphose. Wie bei all seinen Projekten hat Jacob Laws versucht, die Geschichte seines Kunden mit Hilfe von Design zu erzählen - mit einem einzigartigen Ergebnis. Eine Reihe von Epochen und internationalen Stilen finden in diesem informellen, weltoffenen und anspruchsvollen Raum bequem Platz. Ein Herrenanzug aus Wollstoff wurde als Wandverkleidung verwendet, ergänzt durch offene Etagentürme aus geschwärztem Stahl und Holz, die in einem Designer Showhouse in San Francisco gefunden wurden.

Cette chambre d'adolescente devenue bureau de retraité est une véritable métamorphose masculine. Comme pour tous ses projets, Jacob Laws a tenté de raconter l'histoire de son client en utilisant le design comme moyen d'expression, avec un résultat unique. Un éventail d'époques et de styles internationaux se côtoient confortablement dans cet espace informel, mondain et sophistiqué. Un tissu de costume en laine pour homme est transformé en revêtement mural, complété par des tours d'étagères ouvertes en acier noirci et en bois, trouvées dans un salon de design de San Francisco.

Este dormitorio de chica adolescente convertido en estudio para jubilados es una auténtica metamorfosis masculina. Como en todos sus proyectos, Jacob Laws trató de contar la historia de su cliente utilizando el diseño como medio y con un resultado único. Un abanico de épocas y estilos internacionales conviven cómodamente en este espacio informal, mundano y sofisticado. La tela de los trajes de lana para hombres se convierte en revestimiento de las paredes, complementado por torres de estanterías abiertas de acero y madera ennegrecidas a medida, encontradas en una exposición de diseño de San Francisco.

CORONA
THE SECRET PILGRIM

PRICE ROAD

ST. LOUIS, MISSOURI, UNITED STATES

PHOTOS© MEGAN LORENZ, SUZY GORMAN

This work-from-home office space is situated in the formal entry foyer of a modest 1920s home and serves as an informal work space and a place to host in-person meetings with clients and staff. Setting the tone for the rest of the home, the design of this home office needed to be functional and conducive to productivity. One side of the space is dominated by open built-in bookcases painted in chartreuse lacquer, with hidden lateral files retrofitted behind cabinet doors. The other side of the office space has a more intimate feeling and is painted in a dark "Black Fox" colour. The minimal office desk with naked sides blends in with the background, while the wingback chair in Dedar velvet and the same chartreuse green as the informal space acts as a visual connection between the two areas. A black-and-white photography by Stanley Feldman and an exterior coach light add an original touch to the space.

Ce bureau à domicile est situé dans le hall d'entrée formel d'une modeste maison des années 1920 et sert d'espace de travail informel et d'endroit pour organiser des réunions en personne avec les clients et le personnel. Donnant le ton au reste, l'aménagement de ce bureau à domicile devait être fonctionnel et propice à la productivité. Un côté de l'espace est dominé par des bibliothèques encastrées ouvertes peintes en laque chartreuse, avec des dossiers latéraux cachés installés derrière les portes des armoires. L'autre côté de l'espace de bureau offre une sensation plus intime et est peint dans une couleur sombre « Black Fox ». Le bureau minimal aux côtés nus se fond dans le décor, tandis que le fauteuil à oreilles en velours Dedar et du même vert chartreuse que l'espace informel sert de lien visuel entre les deux zones. Une photographie en noir et blanc de Stanley Feldman et une lampe de carrosse extérieure ajoutent une touche originale.

Dieses Heimbüro befindet sich im formellen Eingangsbereich eines bescheidenen Hauses aus den 1920er Jahren und dient als informeller Arbeitsbereich und als Ort für persönliche Treffen mit Kunden und Mitarbeitern. Das Design dieses Heimbüros war tonangebend und sollte funktional und produktivitätsfördernd sein. Eine Seite des Raums wird von offenen, in Chartreuse lackierten Einbaubücherregalen dominiert, in denen hinter Schranktüren versteckte Seitenordner nachgerüstet wurden. Die andere Seite des Büroraums wirkt intimer und ist in der dunklen Farbe „Black Fox" gehalten. Der minimale Schreibtisch mit nackten Seiten fügt sich in den Hintergrund ein, während der Ohrensessel aus Dedar-Samt in demselben Chartreuse-Grün wie der informelle Raum als visuelle Verbindung zwischen den beiden Bereichen dient. Eine Schwarz-Weiß-Fotografie von Stanley Feldman und eine Außenleuchte für den Bus setzen originelle Akzente.

Esta oficina para trabajar desde casa está situada en el vestíbulo formal de una modesta casa de los años 20 y sirve como espacio de trabajo informal y como lugar para celebrar reuniones en persona con clientes y empleados. El diseño de esta oficina debía ser funcional y propiciar la productividad. Uno de los lados del espacio está dominado por librerías empotradas abiertas pintadas en laca chartreuse, con archivos laterales ocultos instalados detrás de las puertas de los armarios. El otro lado del espacio de la oficina tiene una sensación más íntima y está pintado en un color oscuro «Black Fox». El mínimo escritorio con los lados desnudos se funde con el fondo, mientras que la silla con respaldo en terciopelo Dedar y el mismo verde chartreuse del espacio informal actúa como conexión visual entre las dos zonas. Una fotografía en blanco y negro de Stanley Feldman y una luz de carroza exterior añaden un toque original.

Janis Joplin
TO DRUNK TO FUC

JANNAT VASI INTERIOR DESIGN

JANNAT VASI

www.jannatvasi.com

Based in Mumbai, India, Jannat Vasi Interior Design is a multi-disciplinary boutique practice specialised in luxury residential projects, as well as commercial and hospitality interiors. Jannat Vasi's modern aesthetic approach and the use of a bold palette, embossed textures and unique surface treatments has received international acclaim. For Jannat Vasi, the design strategy starts with the human experience. Her spaces are a reflection of what she senses, feels and sees in her life and travels around the world. The result is unique spaces which are functional and characterised by a strong personality.

Jannat Vasi Interior Design mit Sitz in Mumbai, Indien, ist ein multidisziplinäres Studio, das sich auf luxuriöse Wohnprojekte sowie kommerzielle und gastgewerbliche Inneneinrichtungen spezialisiert hat. Jannat Vasis moderner ästhetischer Ansatz und die Verwendung kühner Farbpaletten, geprägter Texturen und einzigartiger Oberflächenbehandlungen haben internationale Auszeichnungen erhalten. Für Jannat Vasi beginnt die Designstrategie mit der menschlichen Erfahrung. Ihre Räume spiegeln das wider, was sie in ihrem Leben und auf ihren Reisen um die Welt wahrnimmt, fühlt und sieht. Das Ergebnis sind einzigartige, funktionale Räume mit einer starken Persönlichkeit.

POP ART HOUSE

SKY GARDEN

Basé à Mumbai, en Inde, Jannat Vasi Interior Design est un studio pluridisciplinaire spécialisé dans les projets résidentiels de luxe ainsi que dans les intérieurs commerciaux et d'accueil. L'approche esthétique moderne de Jannat Vasi et l'utilisation de palettes audacieuses, de textures en relief et de traitements de surface uniques ont reçu des éloges internationaux. Pour Jannat Vasi, la stratégie de conception commence par l'expérience humaine. Ses espaces sont le reflet de ce qu'elle perçoit, ressent et voit dans sa vie et dans ses voyages autour du monde. Il en résulte des espaces uniques, fonctionnels et dotés d'une forte personnalité.

Con sede en Mumbai (India), Jannat Vasi Interior Design es un estudio multidisciplinar especializado en proyectos residenciales de lujo, así como en interiores comerciales y de hostelería. El enfoque estético moderno de Jannat Vasi y el uso de una paleta audaz, texturas en relieve y tratamientos de superficie únicos han recibido elogios internacionales. Para Jannat Vasi, la estrategia de diseño comienza con la experiencia humana. Sus espacios son un reflejo de lo que percibe, siente y ve en su vida y en sus viajes por el mundo. El resultado son espacios únicos, funcionales y con una fuerte personalidad.

POP ART HOUSE

MUMBAI, INDIA

PHOTOS © SULEIMAN MERCHANT

The clients of this three-storey home in Mumbai's luxe Peddar Road suburb of Mumbai are three brothers from a well-known family of mill owners in India's largest city. As is common in large industrial houses in India, the three brothers decided to live together, each one occupying a separate floor together with their wife and children. Aiming to reflect the clients' personality, Jannat Vasi was inspired by their collection of iconic pop art and rare collectibles and proposed a combination of chromatic patterns and colour blocking. Sculptural display systems are weaved into the design of this seven-bedroom home to showcase the owner's unique and beautiful pieces, including limited-edition art and books.

Die Bauherren dieses dreistöckigen Hauses im gehobenen Viertel Peddar Road in Mumbai sind drei Brüder aus einer bekannten Familie von Mühlenbesitzern in Indiens größter Stadt. Wie in den großen Industriegebäuden des Landes üblich, beschlossen die drei Brüder, zusammenzuleben, wobei jeder mit seiner Frau und seinen Kindern eine eigene Etage bewohnte. Mit dem Ziel, die Persönlichkeit der Kunden widerzuspiegeln, ließ sich Jannat Vasi von seiner Sammlung ikonischer Pop-Art und seltener Sammlerstücke inspirieren und schlug eine Kombination aus Farbmustern und Colourblocking vor. Skulpturale Ausstellungssysteme wurden in das Design dieses Hauses mit sieben Schlafzimmern integriert, um die einzigartigen und schönen Stücke des Eigentümers zu präsentieren, darunter Kunstwerke und Bücher in limitierter Auflage.

Les clients de cette maison de trois étages située dans le quartier huppé de Peddar Road à Mumbai sont trois frères issus d'une famille de propriétaires de moulins bien connue dans la plus grande ville de l'Inde. Comme il est d'usage dans les grandes maisons industrielles du pays, les trois frères ont décidé de vivre ensemble, chacun occupant un étage séparé avec sa femme et ses enfants. Dans le but de refléter la personnalité des clients, Jannat Vasi s'est inspiré de sa collection de pop art iconique et d'objets de collection rares et a proposé une combinaison de motifs chromatiques et de blocs de couleurs. Des systèmes d'exposition sculpturaux ont été intégrés au design de cette maison de sept chambres pour mettre en valeur les pièces uniques et magnifiques du propriétaire, notamment des œuvres d'art et des livres à tirage limité.

Los clientes de esta casa de tres plantas situada en el lujoso barrio de Peddar Road, en Bombay, son tres hermanos de una conocida familia de propietarios de molinos de la mayor ciudad de la India. Como es habitual en las grandes casas industriales del país, los tres hermanos decidieron vivir juntos, ocupando cada uno una planta independiente junto con su mujer y sus hijos. Con el objetivo de reflejar la personalidad de los clientes, Jannat Vasi se inspiró en su colección de arte pop icónico y objetos raros de colección y propuso una combinación de patrones cromáticos y bloqueo de color. En el diseño de esta casa de siete dormitorios se han integrado sistemas de exposición escultórica para mostrar las piezas únicas y hermosas del propietario, entre las que se incluyen obras de arte y libros de edición limitada.

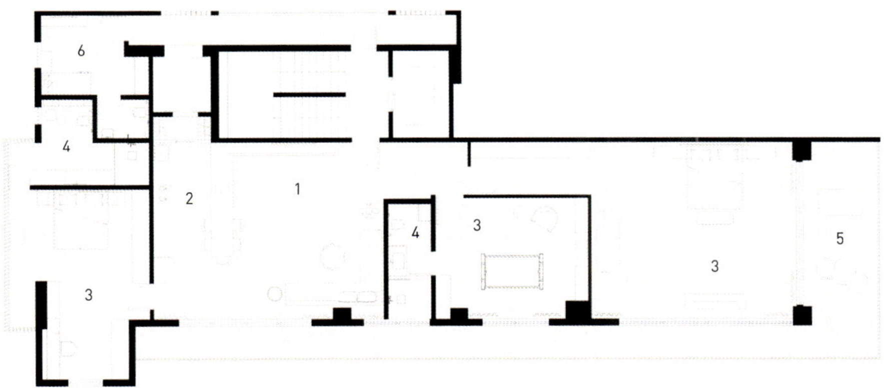

1. Living area
2. Kitchen
3. Bedroom
4. Bathroom
5. Balcony
6. Servants quarter

Second level plan

1. Bedroom
2. Walk-in wardrobe
3. Bathroom
4. Servants quarter
5. Refuge area

First level plan

SKY GARDEN

MUMBAI, INDIA

PHOTOS © ASHISH SAHI

Situated in Mumbai, Jannat Vasi was given a unique chance to design a one-of-a kind apartment for a young couple looking to turn an empty terrace floor into an elegant and homely space. Jannat Vasi custom-designed every detail of the apartment, from the marble inlay to the tailor-made furniture and landscaping. The apartment is infused with her signature style, featuring bold colours and embossed textures. A large part of this 185 m^2 home is dedicated to the spacious master suite, walk-in wardrobe and master bedroom. Carved out of the bedroom space is a beautiful corner office with accents of gold, which imbue a sense of luxury and tradition at the same time.

Das in Mumbai ansässige Unternehmen Jannat Vasi hatte die einmalige Gelegenheit, eine einzigartige Wohnung für ein junges Paar zu entwerfen, das eine leere Terrassenwohnung in einen stilvollen und einladenden Raum verwandeln wollte. Jannat Vasi hat jedes Detail der Wohnung individuell gestaltet, von den Marmorintarsien bis hin zu den maßgeschneiderten Möbeln und der Gartengestaltung. Die Wohnung ist von ihrem unverkennbaren Stil geprägt, mit leuchtenden Farben und geprägten Strukturen. Ein großer Teil der 185 m^2 großen Wohnfläche ist der geräumigen Master-Suite, dem Ankleidezimmer und dem Hauptschlafzimmer gewidmet, das mit einem wunderschönen Eckbüro mit vergoldeten Details ausgestattet ist, die ein Gefühl von Luxus und Tradition vermitteln.

Situé à Mumbai, Jannat Vasi a eu l'occasion unique de concevoir un appartement unique pour un jeune couple qui souhaitait transformer un appartement terrasse vide en un espace élégant et accueillant. Jannat Vasi a conçu chaque détail de l'appartement, des incrustations de marbre au mobilier sur mesure et à l'aménagement paysager. L'appartement est imprégné de son style caractéristique, avec des couleurs vives et des textures en relief. Une grande partie de cette maison de 185 m^2 est consacrée à la suite principale spacieuse, au dressing et à la chambre principale, qui comporte un beau bureau d'angle avec des détails dorés, créant un sentiment de luxe et de tradition.

Situado en Mumbai, Jannat Vasi tuvo la oportunidad única de diseñar un apartamento singular para una joven pareja que quería convertir un piso vacío en una terraza en un espacio elegante y acogedor. Jannat Vasi diseñó a medida cada detalle del apartamento, desde las incrustaciones de mármol hasta los muebles hechos a medida y el paisajismo. El apartamento está impregnado de su estilo característico, con colores vivos y texturas en relieve. Una gran parte de esta vivienda de 185 m^2 está dedicada a la espaciosa suite principal, al vestidor y al dormitorio principal, en el que se encuentra un precioso despacho de esquina con detalles dorados, que imprimen una sensación de lujo y tradición.

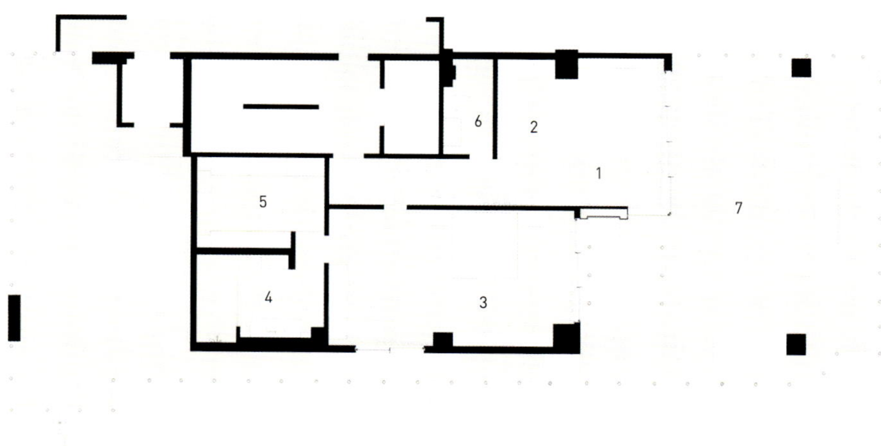

1. Living room
2. Kitchen
3. Bedroom
4. Bathroom
5. Walk-in wardrobe
6. Powder room
7. Terrace

Floor plan

JUAN ALBERTO ANDRADE, MARÍA JOSÉ VÁSCONES

JUAN ALBERTO ANDRADE,
MARÍA JOSÉ VÁSCONES,
CUQUI RODRÍGUEZ

www.juanalbertoandrade.ec

Ecuadorian architects Juan Alberto Andrade and María José Váscones have come together to work on a number of diverse projects. María José Váscones graduated from Universidad Católica de Santiago de Guayaquil in 2021 and is inspired by a wide range of artistic fields, from architecture, art and interior design to film and fashion. Juan Alberto Andrade, architect and photographer, specialises in architecture, photography and communications and co-runs JAG Studio, offering communications and photography services in Ecuador, Mexico and Bolivia.

Die ecuadorianischen Architekten Juan Alberto Andrade und María José Váscones haben sich zusammengetan, um an einer Reihe unterschiedlicher Projekte zu arbeiten. María José Váscones schloss 2021 ihr Studium an der Universidad Católica de Santiago de Guayaquil ab und lässt sich von einem breiten Spektrum künstlerischer Bereiche inspirieren, von Architektur, Kunst und Innenarchitektur bis hin zu Film und Mode. Juan Alberto Andrade, Architekt und Fotograf, hat sich auf Architektur, Fotografie und Kommunikation spezialisiert und ist Mitbetreiber des JAG Studios, das Kommunikations- und Fotodienstleistungen in Ecuador, Mexiko und Bolivien anbietet.

DOMÉSTICO

Les architectes équatoriens Juan Alberto Andrade et María José Váscones se sont réunis pour travailler sur un certain nombre de projets divers. Diplômée de l'Universidad Católica de Santiago de Guayaquil en 2021, María José Váscones s'inspire d'un large éventail de domaines artistiques, de l'architecture, de l'art et de la décoration d'intérieur au cinéma et à la mode. Juan Alberto Andrade, architecte et photographe, est spécialisé dans l'architecture, la photographie et la communication et codirige JAG Studio, qui propose des services de communication et de photographie en Équateur, au Mexique et en Bolivie.

Los arquitectos ecuatorianos Juan Alberto Andrade y María José Váscones se han unido para trabajar en diversos proyectos. María José Váscones se graduó en la Universidad Católica de Santiago de Guayaquil en 2021 y se inspira en una amplia gama de campos artísticos, desde la arquitectura, el arte y el diseño de interiores hasta el cine y la moda. Juan Alberto Andrade, arquitecto y fotógrafo, está especializado en arquitectura, fotografía y comunicación y codirige el estudio JAG, que ofrece servicios de comunicación y fotografía en Ecuador, México y Bolivia.

DOMÉSTICO

QUITO, ECUADOR

PHOTOS © JAG STUDIO

This tiny, 29 m^2 apartment is located inside the Qorner building, the apartment tower designed by Moshe Safdie & Uribe Schwarzkopf near La Carolina Park in Quito, Ecuador. Asked to create a flexible home for an active middle-aged woman, without foregoing comfort and basic living amenities, Juan Alberto Andrade and María José Váscones created a floor-to-ceiling unit that condenses all functions for everyday living. The so-called "habitable artifact" made of water-resistant melamine boards, holds all activities, services and equipment for everyday living, such as the kitchen, storage, laundry, bedroom, and working, dining and entertaining. The unit stretches along the walls of the apartment, containing, on one side of the room, a bed and desk/table, with a door in the corner opening into a small bathroom with shower, sink and toilet. Green metal shelves above add both storage and some colour to the interior.

Diese winzige, 29 m^2 große Wohnung befindet sich im Qorner-Gebäude, dem von Moshe Safdie & Uribe Schwarzkopf entworfenen Wohnturm in der Nähe des La Carolina Parks in Quito, Ecuador. Juan Alberto Andrade und María José Váscones sollten ein flexibles Zuhause für eine aktive Frau mittleren Alters schaffen, ohne dabei auf Komfort und grundlegende Annehmlichkeiten zu verzichten, und entwarfen eine raumhohe Einheit, die alle Funktionen des täglichen Lebens in sich vereint. Das so genannte „bewohnbare Artefakt" aus wasserfesten Melaminplatten beherbergt alle Aktivitäten, Dienstleistungen und Geräte für das tägliche Leben, wie Küche, Lager, Wäscherei, Schlafzimmer, Arbeits-, Ess- und Unterhaltungsbereich. Wenn man das Studio betritt, erstreckt sich die Einheit entlang der Wände der Wohnung und enthält auf einer Seite des Raumes ein Bett und einen Schreibtisch/Tisch, während eine Tür in der Ecke in ein kleines Badezimmer mit Dusche, Waschbecken und Toilette führt. Darüber befinden sich grüne Metallregale, die sowohl Stauraum als auch etwas Farbe ins Innere bringen.

Ce minuscule appartement de 29 m^2 est situé à l'intérieur du bâtiment Qorner, la tour d'appartements conçue par Moshe Safdie & Uribe Schwarzkopf près du parc La Carolina à Quito, en Équateur. Chargés de créer un logement flexible pour une femme active d'âge moyen, sans renoncer au confort et aux commodités de base, Juan Alberto Andrade et María José Váscones ont créé une unité du sol au plafond qui condense toutes les fonctions de la vie quotidienne. Ce que l'on appelle « l'artefact habitable », fait de panneaux de mélamine résistants à l'eau, contient toutes les activités, les services et les équipements nécessaires à la vie quotidienne, tels que la cuisine, le stockage, la buanderie, la chambre à coucher, le travail, les repas et les divertissements. L'unité s'étend le long des murs de l'appartement, contenant, d'un côté de la pièce, un lit et un bureau/table, avec une porte dans le coin s'ouvrant sur une petite salle de bain avec douche, lavabo et toilettes. Au-dessus, des étagères métalliques vertes ajoutent à la fois du rangement et de la couleur à l'intérieur.

Este diminuto apartamento de 29 m^2 se encuentra dentro del edificio Qorner, la torre de apartamentos diseñada por Moshe Safdie & Uribe Schwarzkopf cerca del parque La Carolina en Quito, Ecuador. Con el objetivo de crear una vivienda flexible para una mujer activa de mediana edad, sin renunciar a la comodidad y a los servicios básicos, Juan Alberto Andrade y María José Váscones crearon una unidad de suelo a techo que condensa todas las funciones para la vida cotidiana. El llamado «artefacto habitable», fabricado con tableros de melamina resistentes al agua, alberga todas las actividades, servicios y equipamientos para la vida cotidiana, como la cocina, el almacén, la lavandería, el dormitorio, y el trabajo, la cena y el entretenimiento. El mueble se extiende a lo largo de las paredes del apartamento, conteniendo, en un lado de la habitación, una cama y un escritorio/mesa, con una puerta en la esquina que da paso a un pequeño baño con ducha, lavabo e inodoro. Las estanterías metálicas de color verde que se encuentran encima añaden almacenamiento y algo de color al interior.

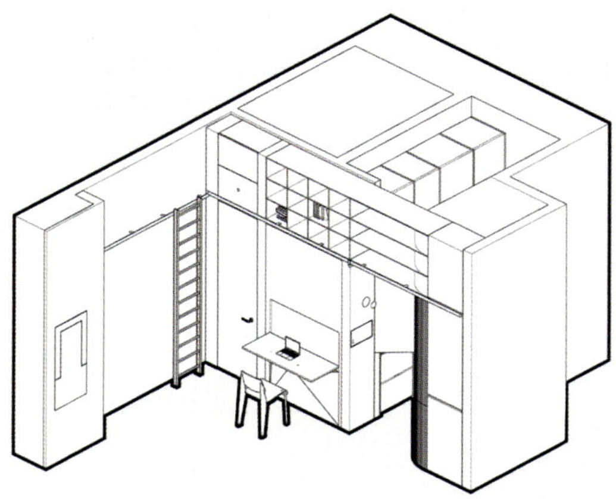

Scenario

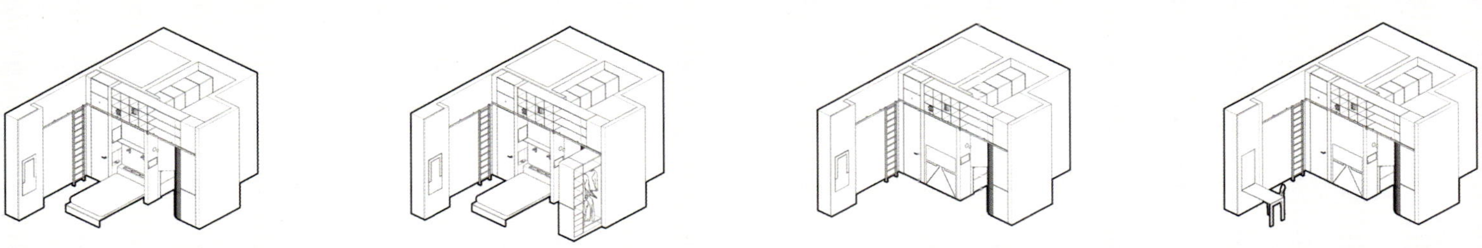

Scenarios

KOTO STUDIO

JOHNATHON LITTLE, ZOË LITTLE, THEO DALES

www.kotodesign.co.uk

Husband-and-wife duo Johnathon and Zoë Little founded Koto in January 2018 after a decade of living on the shores of the Nordic fjords, where they fostered a deep appreciation of the local aesthetic and environment. Co-founder Theo Dales joined them a year later and today Koto ('cosy home' in Finnish) is known for high-quality and energy-neutral prefabricated homes and cabins. Koto takes inspiration from the ethos of Scandinavian design, culture and way of living, as well the minimalist world of Japanese design. Each and every Koto home embodies the dynamic relationship between nature and quality design and is designed for living and enjoying time with friends and family. Each home is built with the utmost respect for the environment and people working together with Koto.

Das Ehepaar Johnathon und Zoë Little gründete Koto im Januar 2018, nachdem sie ein Jahrzehnt an den Küsten der nordischen Fjorde gelebt hatten, wo sie eine tiefe Wertschätzung für die lokale Ästhetik und Umwelt entwickelten. Mitbegründer Theo Dales stieß ein Jahr später dazu, und heute ist Koto („gemütliches Haus" auf Finnisch) für seine hochwertigen, energieneutralen Fertighäuser und Hütten bekannt. Koto ist vom Geist des skandinavischen Designs, der skandinavischen Kultur und Lebensart sowie von der minimalistischen Welt des japanischen Designs inspiriert. Jedes einzelne Haus von Koto verkörpert die dynamische Beziehung zwischen Natur und hochwertigem Design und ist für das Wohnen und Genießen von Zeit mit Freunden und Familie konzipiert. Jedes Haus wird mit größtem Respekt für die Umwelt und die Menschen, die mit Koto arbeiten, gebaut.

SCULPTURE CABIN

Le duo mari et femme Johnathon et Zoë Little a fondé Koto en janvier 2018 après une décennie passée sur les rives des fjords nordiques, où ils ont nourri une profonde appréciation de l'esthétique et de l'environnement locaux. Le cofondateur Theo Dales les a rejoints un an plus tard et aujourd'hui, Koto (« maison confortable » en finnois) est connu pour ses maisons et cabanes préfabriquées de haute qualité et neutres en énergie. Koto s'inspire de l'esprit du design, de la culture et du mode de vie scandinaves, ainsi que de l'univers minimaliste du design japonais. Chaque maison Koto incarne la relation dynamique entre la nature et un design de qualité et est conçue pour vivre et profiter du temps avec les amis et la famille. Chaque maison est construite dans le plus grand respect de l'environnement et des personnes qui travaillent avec Koto.

El dúo de marido y mujer Johnathon y Zoë Little fundaron Koto en enero de 2018 tras una década viviendo en las costas de los fiordos nórdicos, donde fomentaron un profundo aprecio por la estética y el entorno locales. El cofundador Theo Dales se unió a ellos un año después y hoy Koto («hogar acogedor» en finlandés) es conocido por sus casas y cabañas prefabricadas de alta calidad y neutralidad energética. Koto se inspira en el espíritu del diseño, la cultura y el modo de vida escandinavos, así como en el mundo minimalista del diseño japonés. Todas y cada una de las casas de Koto encarnan la relación dinámica entre la naturaleza y el diseño de calidad y están diseñadas para vivir y disfrutar del tiempo con los amigos y la familia. Cada casa se construye con el máximo respeto al medio ambiente y a las personas que colaboran con Koto.

SCULPTURE CABIN

NEW ART CENTRE, SALISBURY, UNITED KINGDOM

PHOTOS © EDVINAS BRUZAS

Commissioned by the New Art Centre, a gallery and sculpture park in Salisbury, England, this geometric, modular workspace reimagines where, and how, we work. Inspired by the gallery's sculpture garden and the ancient Japanese philosophy of Wabi Sabi, the Sculpture Cabin connects with the surrounding nature and serves as a place of deep work and meditation. The elegant, functional and carbon-neutral structure is built form natural materials and can work both on- and off-grid. A large window on one side of the structure offers uninterrupted views over any landscape and direct access to nature.

Im Auftrag des New Art Centre, einer Galerie und eines Skulpturenparks in Salisbury, England, hat dieser geometrische, modulare Arbeitsraum den Ort und die Art, wie wir arbeiten, neu definiert. Inspiriert vom Skulpturengarten der Galerie und der alten japanischen Philosophie des Wabi Sabi, verbindet sich die Skulpturenhütte mit der umgebenden Natur und dient als Ort der Arbeit und Meditation. Die elegante, funktionale und kohlenstoffneutrale Struktur besteht aus natürlichen Materialien und kann sowohl mit als auch ohne Netzanschluss betrieben werden. Ein großes Fenster auf einer Seite des Gebäudes bietet einen ungehinderten Blick auf die Landschaft und einen direkten Zugang zur Natur.

Commandé par le New Art Centre, une galerie et un parc de sculptures à Salisbury, en Angleterre, cet espace de travail géométrique et modulaire repense l'endroit et la manière dont nous travaillons. Inspirée du jardin de sculptures de la galerie et de l'ancienne philosophie japonaise du Wabi Sabi, la Cabane à Sculptures se connecte à la nature environnante et sert de lieu de travail et de méditation. Cette structure élégante, fonctionnelle et neutre en carbone est construite à partir de matériaux naturels et peut fonctionner à la fois sur et hors réseau. Une grande fenêtre sur un côté de la structure offre une vue ininterrompue sur n'importe quel paysage et un accès direct à la nature.

Por encargo del New Art Centre, una galería y parque de esculturas de Salisbury (Inglaterra), este espacio de trabajo geométrico y modular re imagina dónde y cómo trabajamos. Inspirada en el jardín de esculturas de la galería y en la antigua filosofía japonesa del Wabi Sabi, la Cabaña Escultura conecta con la naturaleza circundante y sirve como lugar de trabajo y meditación. La estructura, elegante, funcional y neutra en emisiones de carbono, está construida con materiales naturales y puede funcionar tanto dentro como fuera de la red. Un gran ventanal en un lado de la estructura ofrece vistas ininterrumpidas de cualquier paisaje y acceso directo a la naturaleza.

MARTIN HOPP ARCHITECT (MHA)

MARTIN HOPP

www.martinhopp.com

Founded in 2013, Martin Hopp Architect (MHA) is a New-York based architecture firm based focused on the design of educational facilities, civic project, healthy building and new sustainable approaches, including circular construction and timber structural systems. Martin Hopp trained and practised in the UK and Germany, and brings the forward-looking sustainability, healthy building, and circular construction approaches pioneered in Europe to a new level in his projects. As one of the first firms to use cross-laminated timber as an alternative to steel or concrete structures in New York, MHA has delivered award-winning projects based on improving environmental quality and user experience.

Martin Hopp Architect (MHA) wurde 2013 gegründet und ist ein in New York ansässiges Architekturbüro, das sich auf die Gestaltung von Bildungseinrichtungen, städtischen Projekten, gesundem Bauen und neuen nachhaltigen Ansätzen, einschließlich Kreislaufbauweise und Holzbausystemen, konzentriert. Martin Hopp wurde im Vereinigten Königreich und in Deutschland ausgebildet und praktiziert. In seinen Projekten bringt er die zukunftsweisenden Ansätze der Nachhaltigkeit, des gesunden Bauens und der Kreislaufbauweise, die in Europa Pionierarbeit geleistet haben, auf ein neues Niveau. Als eines der ersten Unternehmen, das in New York Brettsperrholz als Alternative zu Stahl- oder Betonkonstruktionen einsetzte, hat MHA preisgekrönte Projekte realisiert, die auf der Verbesserung der Umweltqualität und der Nutzererfahrung basieren.

CHELSEA BASEMENT

Fondé en 2013, Martin Hopp Architect (MHA) est un cabinet d'architecture basé à New-York axé sur la conception d'installations éducatives, de projets civiques, de bâtiments sains et de nouvelles approches durables, notamment la construction circulaire et les systèmes structurels en bois. Martin Hopp a été formé et a exercé au Royaume-Uni et en Allemagne. Dans ses projets, il porte à un niveau supérieur les approches de la durabilité, de la construction saine et de la construction circulaire qui ont fait leurs preuves en Europe. Étant l'une des premières entreprises à utiliser le bois lamellé-croisé comme alternative aux structures en acier ou en béton à New York, MHA a réalisé des projets primés basés sur l'amélioration de la qualité environnementale et de l'expérience des utilisateurs.

Fundado en 2013, Martin Hopp Architect (MHA) es un estudio de arquitectura con sede en Nueva York centrado en el diseño de instalaciones educativas, proyectos cívicos, construcciones saludables y nuevos enfoques sostenibles, incluyendo la construcción circular y los sistemas estructurales de madera. Martin Hopp se formó y ejerció en el Reino Unido y Alemania, y lleva a un nuevo nivel en sus proyectos los enfoques de sostenibilidad, construcción saludable y construcción circular pioneros en Europa. Como una de las primeras empresas en utilizar la madera laminada cruzada como alternativa a las estructuras de acero u hormigón en Nueva York, MHA ha realizado proyectos premiados basados en la mejora de la calidad ambiental y la experiencia del usuario.

CHELSEA BASEMENT

NEW YORK, UNITED STATES

PHOTOS © FEI LIU

The renovation of this garden-level apartment located in a 1930s apartment building in the Chelsea neighbourhood aimed at introducing more lightness, joy and purpose. With major structural challenges, as well as limitations in space, MHA used flexible targeted design to create a multi-functional home that reflects today's work/life balance. Using all-white cabinetry and built-in furniture, MHA added brightness and a sense of space to the main living area, which includes the kitchen and living-dining space. On the other side of the kitchen, Martin Hopp and his team turned an oversized closet in the hallway into a unique guest room/home office/storage area. At the end of the day, the neat work desk can be folded away and a custom-built Murphy bed can be pulled down for guests. White oak is used throughout the apartment on floors and walls, and creative lighting strategies, like the backlit shelving in the bathroom, add a feeling of warmth and function to the space. Space-saving sliding doors allow for more privacy when needed.

Die Renovierung dieser Wohnung mit Gartengeschoss in einem Wohnhaus aus den 1930er Jahren im Stadtteil Chelsea hatte zum Ziel, mehr Leichtigkeit, Freude und Zweckmäßigkeit zu schaffen. Angesichts der großen baulichen Herausforderungen und des begrenzten Raums nutzte MHA ein flexibles, zielgerichtetes Design, um eine multifunktionale Wohnung zu schaffen, die die heutige Work-Life-Balance widerspiegelt.Durch die Verwendung von komplett weißen Schränken und Einbaumöbeln verlieh MHA dem Hauptwohnbereich, der die Küche und den Wohn-Essbereich umfasst, Helligkeit und ein Gefühl von Raum. Auf der anderen Seite der Küche verwandelten Martin Hopp und sein Team einen übergroßen Wandschrank im Flur in ein einzigartiges Gästezimmer/Heimbüro/Stauraum. Am Ende des Tages kann der ordentliche Arbeitstisch weggeklappt und ein maßgefertigtes Klappbett für Gäste ausgezogen werden. In der gesamten Wohnung wurde weißes Eichenholz für Böden und Wände verwendet, und kreative Beleuchtungsstrategien, wie die hinterleuchteten Regale im Badezimmer, verleihen dem Raum ein Gefühl von Wärme und Funktion. Platzsparende Schiebetüren sorgen bei Bedarf für mehr Privatsphäre.

La rénovation de cet appartement en rez-de-jardin situé dans un immeuble d'habitation des années 1930 dans le quartier de Chelsea visait à introduire plus de légèreté, de joie et d'utilité. Face à des défis structurels majeurs, ainsi qu'à des limitations d'espace, MHA a utilisé un design flexible et ciblé pour créer une maison multifonctionnelle qui reflète l'équilibre entre vie professionnelle et vie privée d'aujourd'hui. En utilisant des armoires entièrement blanches et des meubles intégrés, MHA a ajouté de la luminosité et un sentiment d'espace à la zone de vie principale, qui comprend la cuisine et l'espace salon-salle à manger. De l'autre côté de la cuisine, Martin Hopp et son équipe ont transformé un placard surdimensionné dans le couloir en une chambre d'amis/bureau à domicile/espace de rangement unique. À la fin de la journée, le bureau bien rangé peut être replié et un lit Murphy sur mesure peut être abaissé pour les invités. Le chêne blanc est utilisé dans tout l'appartement, sur les sols et les murs, et des stratégies d'éclairage créatives, comme les étagères rétroéclairées dans la salle de bains, ajoutent un sentiment de chaleur et de fonctionnalité à l'espace. Des portes coulissantes peu encombrantes permettent d'avoir plus d'intimité si nécessaire.

La renovación de este apartamento a nivel del jardín situado en un edificio de apartamentos de la década de 1930 en el barrio de Chelsea tenía como objetivo introducir más ligereza, alegría y propósito. Con importantes retos estructurales, así como con limitaciones de espacio, MHA utilizó un diseño flexible orientado a crear un hogar multifuncional que reflejara el equilibrio actual entre trabajo y vida privada. Utilizando armarios totalmente blancos y muebles empotrados, MHA añadió luminosidad y sensación de espacio a la zona de estar principal, que incluye la cocina y el salón-comedor. Al otro lado de la cocina, Martin Hopp y su equipo convirtieron un armario de gran tamaño en el pasillo en una singular habitación de invitados, despacho y zona de almacenamiento. Al final del día, la mesa de trabajo se puede plegar y una cama Murphy hecha a medida se puede bajar para los invitados. El roble blanco se utiliza en todo el apartamento, tanto en el suelo como en las paredes, y las creativas estrategias de iluminación, como la estantería retroiluminada del baño, añaden una sensación de calidez y funcionalidad al espacio. Las puertas correderas, que ahorran espacio, permiten una mayor privacidad.

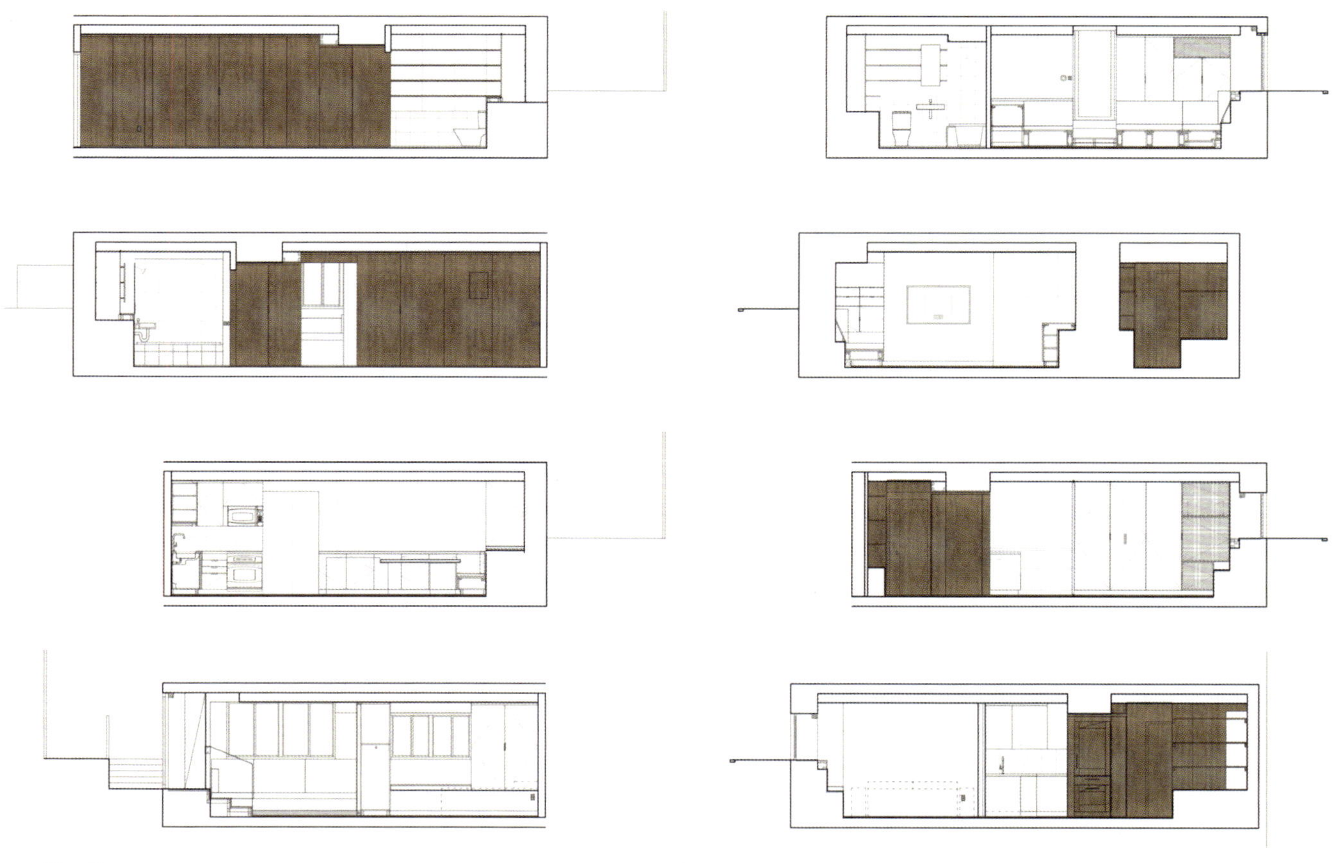

Elevations

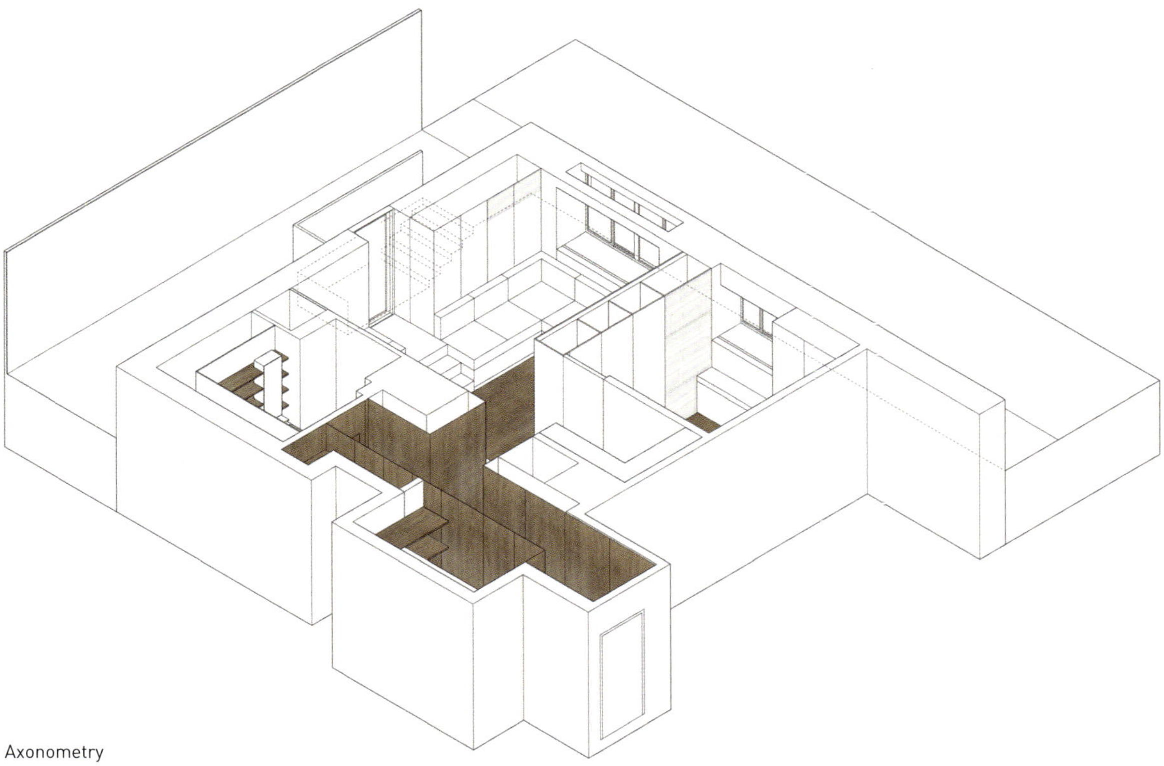

Axonometry

MICHAEL K CHEN ARCHITECTURE (MKCA)

MICHAEL K CHEN

www.mkca.com

Established in 2011, MKCA is a New York-based architecture practice dedicated to producing innovative and superbly crafted work integrating architecture, interior design and product design. MKCA's approach is deeply informed by curiosity and a love of tinkering, of drawing, of collaboration, and of making. Their designs are conceptually and they take on projects at every scale, from large-scale buildings and individual micro apartments to complex urban projects. Internationally renowned as the principal of MKCA, in March 2020 Michael Chen co-founded Design Advocates, a network of independent architecture and design firms collaborating on pro-bono projects for small businesses, institutions, and organizations that serve disadvantaged communities to help them adapt their spaces and operations to adapt to COVID-19 and beyond. Currently, Design Advocates encompasses 120 firms and volunteers working on over 50 projects serving the public good.

MKCA wurde 2011 gegründet und ist ein in New York ansässiges Architekturbüro, das sich der Herstellung innovativer und handwerklich hervorragender Arbeiten verschrieben hat, die Architektur, Innenarchitektur und Produktdesign integrieren. Die Herangehensweise von MKCA ist geprägt von Neugierde und der Liebe zum Basteln, Zeichnen, Zusammenarbeiten und Herstellen. Seine Entwürfe sind konzeptionell und umfassen Projekte in allen Größenordnungen, von großen Gebäuden über einzelne Kleinstwohnungen bis hin zu komplexen Stadtprojekten. Als international anerkannter Leiter von MKCA war Michael Chen im März 2020 Mitbegründer von Design Advocates, einem Netzwerk unabhängiger Architektur- und Designbüros, die bei Pro-bono-Projekten für kleine Unternehmen, Institutionen und Organisationen, die benachteiligten Gemeinschaften dienen, zusammenarbeiten, um ihnen dabei zu helfen, ihre Räume und Abläufe an die COVID-19 und darüber hinaus anzupassen. Design Advocates umfasst derzeit 120 Unternehmen und Freiwillige, die an mehr als 50 Projekten im Dienste des Gemeinwohls arbeiten.

FIVE TO ONE APARTMENT

UNFOLDING APARTMENT

Fondé en 2011, MKCA est un studio d'architecture basé à New York qui se consacre à la production de travaux innovants et superbement réalisés, intégrant l'architecture, l'aménagement intérieur et la conception de produits. L'approche de MKCA est profondément inspirée par la curiosité et l'amour du bricolage, du dessin, de la collaboration et de la fabrication. Ses conceptions sont conceptuelles et portent sur des projets à toutes les échelles, qu'il s'agisse de bâtiments à grande échelle, de micro-appartements individuels ou de projets urbains complexes. Reconnu internationalement en tant que principal chez MKCA, Michael Chen a cofondé en mars 2020 Design Advocates, un réseau de cabinets d'architecture et de design indépendants qui collaborent à des projets pro-bono pour les petites entreprises, les institutions et les organisations au service des communautés défavorisées afin de les aider à adapter leurs espaces et leurs opérations à COVID-19 et au-delà. Design Advocates regroupe actuellement 120 entreprises et bénévoles travaillant sur plus de 50 projets au service du bien public.

Fundado en 2011, MKCA es un estudio de arquitectura con sede en Nueva York dedicado a procucir un trabajo innovador y magníficamente elaborado que integra la arquitectura, el diseño de interiores y el diseño de productos. El enfoque de MKCA está profundamente informado por la curiosidad y el amor por el jugueteo, el dibujo, la colaboración y la fabricación. Sus diseños son conceptuales y se encargan de proyectos a todas las escalas, desde edificios a gran escala y micro apartamentos individuales hasta complejos proyectos urbanos. Reconocido internacionalmente como director de MKCA, en marzo de 2020 Michael Chen co-fundó Design Advocates, una red de estudios independientes de arquitectura y diseño que colaboran en proyectos pro-bono para pequeñas empresas, instituciones y organizaciones que prestan servicios a comunidades desfavorecidas, con el fin de ayudarles a adaptar sus espacios y operaciones para adaptarse a COVID-19 y más allá. En la actualidad, Design Advocates engloba a 120 empresas y voluntarios que trabajan en más de 50 proyectos al servicio del bien público.

FIVE TO ONE APARTMENT

MANHATTAN, NEW YORK, UNITED STATES

PHOTOS © ALAN TANSEY

Situated in a 1920's co-op building in the Gramercy Park, New York, this 5:1 apartment contains the functional and spatial elements for living, working, sleeping, dressing and entertaining within a compact 890 square feet. With several ultra-functional urban micro homes under their belt, MKCA have become experts at creating transforming and moving architecture in small residential spaces. A motorized sliding storage element on one side of this small home, cleverly reveals daytime and night-time zones. By pulling the element away from the wall, the inhabitant can access a dressing room and, when fully extended, fold down a queen-sized bed. The audio-visual and networking components are hidden inside the moving volume, along with extra storage space. When the bed is closed, the bedroom makes room for a large living and working space. A pair of sliding doors reveal an open library, display shelving in powder-coated steel and a small desk. Lower cabinets on either side of the desk house a printer and computer peripherals and office storage.

Situé dans un immeuble coopératif des années 1920 à Gramercy Park, New York, cet appartement 5:1 contient les éléments fonctionnels et spatiaux pour vivre, travailler, dormir, s'habiller et se divertir dans un espace compact de 90 m². Avec plusieurs micro-habitations urbaines ultra-fonctionnelles à son actif, MKCA est devenue experte dans la création d'une architecture transformatrice et émouvante dans de petits espaces résidentiels. Un élément de rangement coulissant motorisé sur un côté de cette petite maison révèle astucieusement les zones de jour et de nuit. En éloignant l'élément du mur, l'habitant peut accéder à un dressing et, lorsqu'il est complètement déployé, rabattre un lit double. Les composants audiovisuels et de réseau sont dissimulés dans le volume mobile, ainsi que des espaces de stockage supplémentaires. Lorsque le lit est fermé, la chambre à coucher laisse place à un vaste espace de vie et de travail. Une paire de portes coulissantes révèle une bibliothèque ouverte, des étagères en acier et un petit bureau. Les placards inférieurs situés de part et d'autre du bureau accueillent une imprimante et des périphériques d'ordinateur, ainsi qu'un espace de rangement pour le bureau.

Diese 5:1-Wohnung befindet sich in einem Genossenschaftsgebäude aus den 1920er Jahren im Gramercy Park, New York. Sie enthält auf kompakten 90 m² die funktionalen und räumlichen Elemente zum Wohnen, Arbeiten, Schlafen, Ankleiden und Unterhalten. Mit mehreren ultra-funktionalen städtischen Mikro-Wohnungen hat MKCA die Fähigkeit erlangt, transformative und bewegende Architektur in kleinen Wohnräumen zu schaffen. Ein motorisiertes, verschiebbares Speicherelement auf einer Seite dieses kleinen Hauses gibt den Blick frei auf die Tag- und Nachtzonen. Schiebt man das Element von der Wand weg, erhält man Zugang zu einem Ankleidezimmer und kann im voll ausgezogenen Zustand ein Doppelbett umklappen. Audio- und Videokomponenten, Netzwerkkomponenten und zusätzlicher Stauraum sind in dem mobilen Volumen verborgen. Wenn das Bett geschlossen ist, gibt das Schlafzimmer den Weg frei für einen großzügigen Wohn- und Arbeitsbereich. Ein Paar Schiebetüren gibt den Blick frei auf ein offenes Bücherregal, Stahlregale und einen kleinen Schreibtisch. Untere Schränke auf beiden Seiten des Schreibtisches bieten Platz für einen Drucker und Computerperipheriegeräte sowie Stauraum für das Büro.

Situado en un edificio cooperativo de 1920 en Gramercy Park, Nueva York, este apartamento 5:1 contiene los elementos funcionales y espaciales para vivir, trabajar, dormir, vestirse y entretenerse dentro de unos compactos 90 m². Con varias micro viviendas urbanas ultrafuncionales en su haber, MKCA se ha convertido en experta en crear una arquitectura transformadora y conmovedora en espacios residenciales pequeños. Un elemento de almacenamiento deslizante motorizado en uno de los lados de esta pequeña casa, revela inteligentemente las zonas de día y de noche. Al apartar el elemento de la pared, el habitante puede acceder a un vestidor y, cuando está totalmente extendido, abatir una cama de matrimonio. Los componentes audiovisuales y de red se ocultan dentro del volumen móvil, junto con un espacio de almacenamiento adicional. Cuando la cama está cerrada, el dormitorio da lugar a un amplio espacio de vida y trabajo. Un par de puertas correderas revelan una biblioteca abierta, estanterías de acero y un pequeño escritorio. Los armarios inferiores situados a ambos lados del escritorio albergan una impresora y periféricos informáticos, así como espacio de almacenamiento para la oficina.

TERMINAL IDENTITY
PLENTY MORE

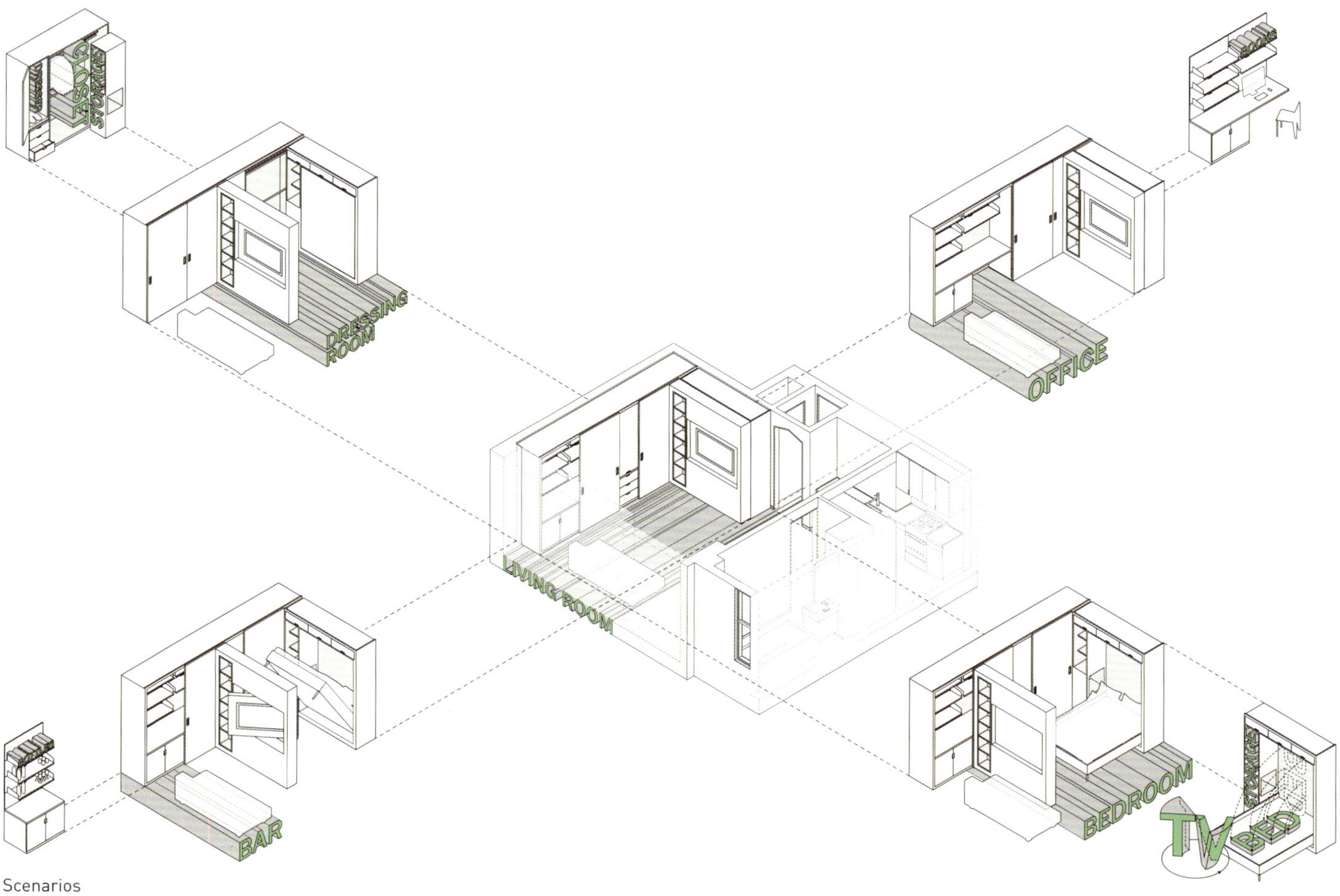

Scenarios

UNFOLDING APARTMENT

MANHATTAN, NEW YORK, UNITED STATES

PHOTOS © ALAN TANSEY

A young single man, who likes to entertain, have houseguests and occasionally works living, needed a clever solution to incorporate all aspects of working, living and entertaining in his compact, 420-square-foot studio in Manhattan. MKCA designed a single oversized volume and inserted it on one end of the space. The custom piece of cabinetry includes a bed, nightstand, closet, home office, library, kitchen storage and lighting. All components of this structure can be unpacked as needed to create a space for sleeping, working, dressing, cooking, dining and entertaining. When not needed, each of the functions can be packed away leaving an open airy and loft-like space. A series of reconfigurable doors and panels slide and pivot open and closed to create the various spaces and transform the studio into whichever use is needed at the time. Spaces can be more or less private thanks to reflective secondary panels, which reveal perforated lacquered metal screens. The mass of blue cabinet is broken by a series of billets recessed into the surface, creating grips and handles to operate the cabinet.

Un jeune célibataire, qui aime recevoir, recevoir des invités et travailler occasionnellement en direct, avait besoin d'une solution intelligente pour intégrer tous les aspects du travail, de la vie et du divertissement dans son studio compact de 40 m² à Manhattan. MKCA a conçu un seul grand volume et l'a inséré à une extrémité de l'espace. Ce meuble sur mesure comprend un lit, une table de chevet, une armoire, un bureau à domicile, une bibliothèque, des rangements pour la cuisine et un éclairage. Tous les éléments de cette structure peuvent être déployés selon les besoins pour créer un espace pour dormir, travailler, s'habiller, cuisiner, manger et recevoir. Lorsque vous n'en avez pas besoin, chacune des fonctions peut être rangée, laissant un espace ouvert et aéré, semblable à un loft. Une série de portes et de panneaux reconfigurables s'ouvrent et se ferment pour créer les différents espaces et transformer le studio en fonction des besoins du moment. Les espaces peuvent être plus ou moins privés grâce aux panneaux secondaires réfléchissants, qui révèlent des écrans en métal laqué perforé. La masse de l'armoire bleue est brisée par une série de petits leviers encastrés dans la surface, qui créent des poignées et des boutons pour faire fonctionner l'armoire.

Ein junger Junggeselle, der gerne Gäste empfängt und gelegentlich live arbeitet, brauchte eine intelligente Lösung, um alle Aspekte von Arbeit, Leben und Unterhaltung in seinem kompakten 40 m² großen Studio in Manhattan, unterzubringen. MKCA entwarf ein einziges großes Volumen und fügte es an einem Ende des Raums ein. Das maßgeschneiderte Möbelstück umfasst ein Bett, einen Nachttisch, einen Kleiderschrank, ein Heimbüro, eine Bibliothek, eine Küchenablage und eine Beleuchtung. Alle Komponenten dieser Struktur können je nach Bedarf eingesetzt werden, um einen Raum zum Schlafen, Arbeiten, Ankleiden, Kochen, Essen und Unterhalten zu schaffen. Wenn sie nicht benötigt werden, können die einzelnen Funktionen verstaut werden, so dass ein offener, luftiger, loftartiger Raum entsteht. Eine Reihe von rekonfigurierbaren Türen und Paneelen, die sich öffnen und schließen lassen, schaffen die verschiedenen Räume und verwandeln das Studio in die jeweils benötigte Nutzung. Die Räume können mehr oder weniger privat sein, dank der reflektierenden Sekundärplatten, die perforierte, lackierte Metallschirme enthüllen. Die Masse des blauen Schranks wird durch eine Reihe von kleinen, in die Oberfläche eingelassenen Hebeln unterbrochen, die Griffe und Knöpfe für die Bedienung des Schranks bilden.

Un joven soltero, al que le gusta tener invitados en casa y ocasionalmente trabajar en directo, necesitaba una solución inteligente para incorporar todos los aspectos del trabajo, la vida y el entretenimiento en su estudio de 40 m2 en Manhattan. MKCA diseñó un único volumen de gran tamaño y lo insertó en un extremo del espacio. La pieza de mobiliario a medida incluye una cama, una mesilla de noche, un armario, una oficina en casa, una biblioteca, almacenamiento en la cocina e iluminación. Todos los componentes de esta estructura pueden desplegarse según sea necesario para crear un espacio para dormir, trabajar, vestirse, cocinar, cenar y entretenerse. Cuando no se necesita, cada una de las funciones puede guardarse dejando un espacio abierto y aireado en forma de loft. Una serie de puertas y paneles reconfigurables se abren y cierran para crear los distintos espacios y transformar el estudio en el uso que se necesite en cada momento. Los espacios pueden ser más o menos privados gracias a los paneles secundarios reflectantes, que dejan ver pantallas metálicas lacadas perforadas. La masa del armario azul se rompe con una serie de pequeñas palancas empotradas en la superficie, que crean asideros y tiradores para manejar el armario.

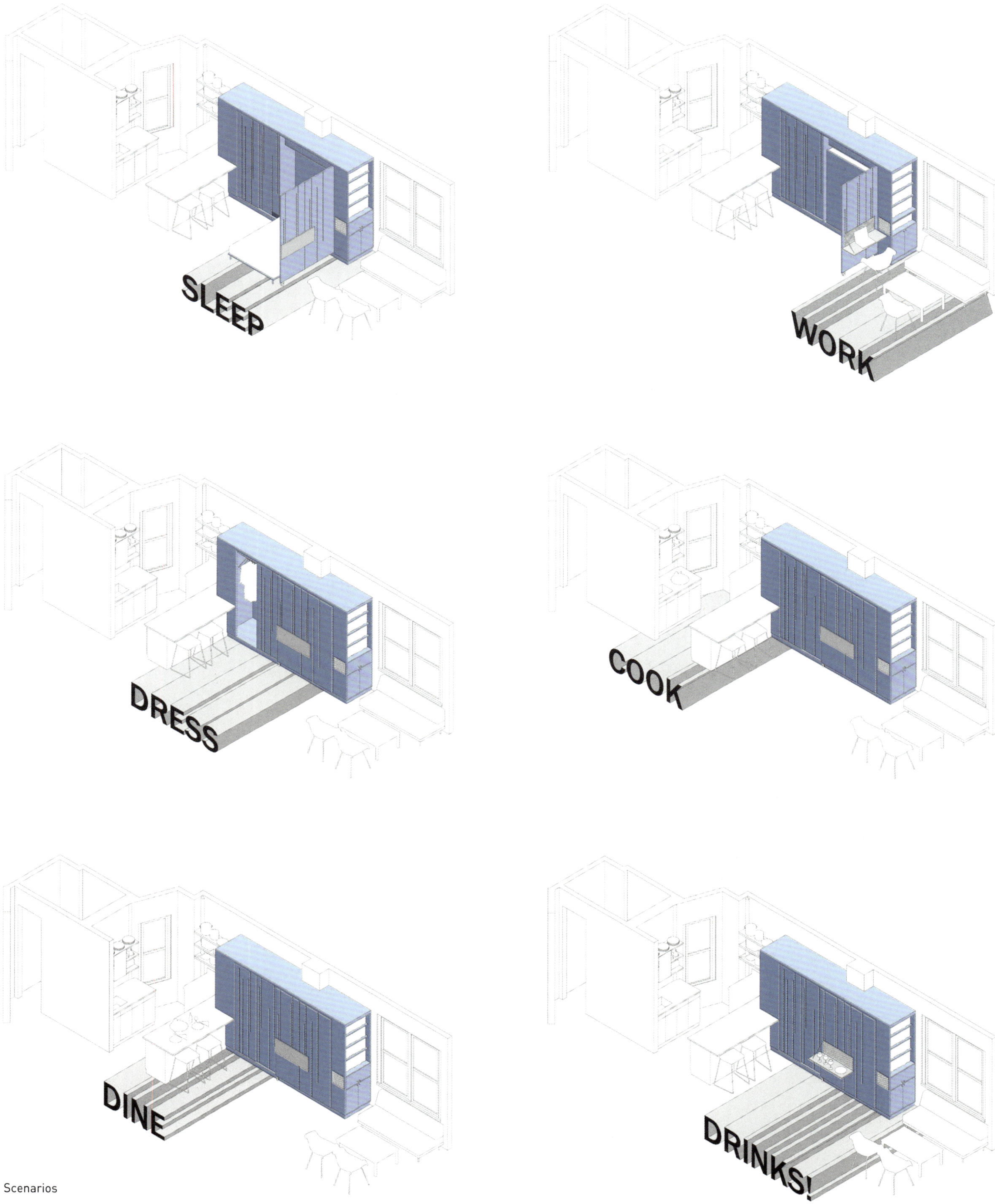

Scenarios

NICOLE BLAIR

NICOLE BLAIR,
STRUCTURES PE,
WISHTREE CARPENTRY

www.nicoleblair.com

Born and raised in Texas, Nicole Blair has received several design awards at local, state and international level. She obtained a Bachelor of Science in Textiles and Apparel from Cornell University (New York) and a Master of Architecture from Rice University (Houston, Texas), and gained early work experience in the NYC offices of Robert A.M. Stern and Peter Eisenman. Today, Nicole Blair's practice (formerly Studio 512) focuses on residential, small commercial and public art building projects. For Nicole Blair the relationship built with clients, artisans, contractors and subcontractors is an important part of building a successful end product.

Nicole Blair ist in Texas geboren und aufgewachsen und hat mehrere Designpreise auf lokaler, nationaler und internationaler Ebene erhalten. Sie erwarb einen Bachelor of Science in Textiles and Apparel an der Cornell University (New York) und einen Master of Architecture an der Rice University (Houston, Texas) und sammelte erste Arbeitserfahrungen in den New Yorker Büros von Robert A.M. Stern und Peter Eisenman. Heute konzentriert sich das Büro von Nicole Blair (ehemals Studio 512) auf Wohn- und kleine Gewerbebauten sowie öffentliche Kunstprojekte. Für Nicole Blair sind die Beziehungen, die sie mit Kunden, Handwerkern, Bauunternehmern und Subunternehmern aufbaut, ein wichtiger Bestandteil eines erfolgreichen Endprodukts.

THE HIVE

Née et élevée au Texas, Nicole Blair a reçu plusieurs prix de design au niveau local, national et international. Elle a obtenu une licence en textile et habillement de l'université Cornell (New York) et une maîtrise en architecture de l'université Rice (Houston, Texas), et a acquis une première expérience professionnelle dans les bureaux new-yorkais de Robert A.M. Stern et Peter Eisenman. Aujourd'hui, le cabinet de Nicole Blair (anciennement Studio 512) se concentre sur des projets de construction résidentiels, de petits commerces et d'art public. Pour Nicole Blair, la relation établie avec les clients, les artisans, les entrepreneurs et les sous-traitants est une partie importante de la construction d'un produit final réussi.

Nacida y criada en Texas, Nicole Blair ha recibido varios premios de diseño a nivel local, estatal e internacional. Se licenció en Ciencias Textiles y de la Confección en la Universidad de Cornell (Nueva York) y obtuvo un máster en Arquitectura en la Universidad de Rice (Houston, Texas), y adquirió experiencia laboral temprana en las oficinas de Robert A.M. Stern y Peter Eisenman en Nueva York. En la actualidad, el estudio de Nicole Blair (antes Studio 512) se centra en proyectos residenciales, pequeños comercios y edificios de arte público. Para Nicole Blair, la relación que se establece con los clientes, los artesanos, los contratistas y los subcontratistas es una parte importante de la construcción de un producto final exitoso.

THE HIVE

AUSTIN, TEXAS, UNITED STATES

PHOTOS © WHIT PRESTON, CASEY DUNN

Limited by building constraints, Nicole Blair took inspiration from Dutch and Japanese architecture, as well as Leonardo da Vinci's The Vitruvian Man, to come up with a creative solution for this one-bedroom 30 m^2 dwelling in East Austin, Texas. Slanting walls help maximize space where it is most needed, like extra counter space in the kitchen and a large built-in desk with cantilevered bookshelf at the top of the stairs. The home office sits at the centre of The Hive and performs multiple functions; the desk acts as a guard rail and wraparound bookcase, as well as a laundry folding counter, and a closet behind the desk hides stackable laundry. The shelves and cabinet fronts in the office and kitchen are longleaf pine material, reclaimed from the walls of a local bungalow. All countertop and flooring material are shou-sugi-ban charred wood, sourced from Delta Millworks in Austin.

Nicole Blair ließ sich von der niederländischen und japanischen Architektur sowie von Leonardo da Vincis Vitruvianischem Menschen inspirieren, um eine kreative Lösung für diese 30 m^2 große Einzimmerwohnung in East Austin, Texas, zu finden. Die schrägen Wände tragen dazu bei, den Platz dort zu maximieren, wo er am meisten gebraucht wird, wie z. B. durch eine zusätzliche Arbeitsfläche in der Küche und einen großen eingebauten Schreibtisch mit auskragendem Bücherregal am oberen Ende der Treppe. Das Home Office befindet sich im Zentrum von The Hive und erfüllt mehrere Funktionen: Der Schreibtisch dient als Geländer und umlaufendes Bücherregal sowie als Wäscheklappe, und ein Schrank hinter dem Schreibtisch verbirgt stapelbare Wäsche. Die Regale und Schrankfronten im Büro und in der Küche bestehen aus Longleaf-Pine-Material, das von den Wänden eines örtlichen Bungalows übernommen wurde. Alle Arbeitsplatten und Bodenbeläge sind aus verkohltem Shou-Sugi-Ban-Holz, das von Delta Millworks in Austin bezogen wurde.

Limitée par les contraintes de construction, Nicole Blair s'est inspirée des architectures hollandaise et japonaise, ainsi que de l'Homme de Vitruve de Léonard de Vinci, pour trouver une solution créative pour cette habitation d'une chambre à coucher de 30 m^2 dans l'est d'Austin, au Texas. Les murs obliques permettent de maximiser l'espace là où il est le plus nécessaire, comme un espace de comptoir supplémentaire dans la cuisine et un grand bureau intégré avec une bibliothèque en porte-à-faux en haut de l'escalier. Le bureau à domicile se trouve au centre de The Hive et remplit plusieurs fonctions : le bureau fait office de garde-corps et de bibliothèque enveloppante, ainsi que de comptoir de pliage du linge, et un placard derrière le bureau cache du linge empilable. Les étagères et les façades des armoires du bureau et de la cuisine sont en pin sylvestre, récupéré sur les murs d'un bungalow local. Tous les comptoirs et revêtements de sol sont en bois calciné *shou-sugi-ban*, provenant de Delta Millworks à Austin.

Limitada por las restricciones de construcción, Nicole Blair se inspiró en la arquitectura holandesa y japonesa, así como en El hombre de Vitruvio de Leonardo da Vinci, para idear una solución creativa para esta vivienda de un dormitorio y 30 m^2 en el este de Austin (Texas). Las paredes inclinadas ayudan a maximizar el espacio donde más se necesita, como el espacio extra de la encimera en la cocina y un gran escritorio empotrado con una estantería en voladizo en la parte superior de la escalera. El espacio de oficina se sitúa en el centro del espacio y cumple múltiples funciones; el escritorio hace las veces de barandilla y librería envolvente, así como de mostrador para doblar la ropa, y un armario detrás del escritorio esconde la ropa apilable. Las estanterías y los frentes de los armarios del despacho y la cocina son de pino de hoja larga, recuperado de las paredes de un bungalow local. Todo el material de la encimera y el suelo es madera carbonizada *shou-sugi-ban*, procedente de Delta Millworks en Austin.

CASTLE WAITING
Inside Outside
Petra Blaisse

PIA CAPDEVILA

PIA CAPDEVILA

www.piacapdevila.com

A perfectionist with a warm, positive and pure personality, Pia Capdevila's qualities shine through in her practical, elegant and natural interior design. Each project is carefully studied and each client gets Pia Capdevila's full attention. She likes to get the know the people who will live in the spaces she designs and wants to understand how they would like to live. Her main objective is to design a home that the client is happy to live in. Based in Barcelona, and with an office in Mallorca, Pia Capdevila and her team take on a wide range of projects, from residential and commercial interiors to exhibition stands, window displays and special events.

Pia Capdevila ist eine Perfektionistin mit einer warmen, positiven und reinen Persönlichkeit. Ihre Qualitäten zeigen sich in ihrer praktischen, eleganten und natürlichen Innenarchitektur. Jedes Projekt wird sorgfältig geprüft, und jeder Kunde erhält Pia Capdevilas volle Aufmerksamkeit. Sie möchte die Menschen kennen lernen, die in den von ihr entworfenen Räumen leben werden, und sie möchte verstehen, wie sie leben möchten. Ihr Hauptziel ist es, ein Haus zu entwerfen, in dem der Kunde gerne lebt. Mit Sitz in Barcelona und einem Büro auf Mallorca führen Pia Capdevila und ihr Team eine breite Palette von Projekten durch, von Wohn- und Geschäftsräumen bis hin zu Messeständen, Schaufenstern und besonderen Veranstaltungen.

GANDUXER APARTMENT

ARIBAU APARTMENT

Perfectionniste, dotée d'une personnalité chaleureuse, positive et pure, les qualités de Pia Capdevila transparaissent dans sa décoration intérieure pratique, élégante et naturelle. Chaque projet est soigneusement étudié et chaque client reçoit toute l'attention de Pia Capdevila. Elle aime apprendre à connaître les personnes qui vivront dans les espaces qu'elle conçoit et veut comprendre comment elles aimeraient vivre. Son principal objectif est de concevoir une maison dans laquelle le client est heureux de vivre. Basée à Barcelone avec un bureau à Majorque, Pia Capdevila et son équipe entreprennent un large éventail de projets, allant des intérieurs résidentiels et commerciaux aux stands d'exposition, aux vitrines et aux événements spéciaux.

Perfeccionista con una personalidad cálida, positiva y pura, las cualidades de Pia Capdevila brillan en su diseño de interiores práctico, elegante y natural. Cada proyecto se estudia cuidadosamente y cada cliente recibe toda la atención de Pia Capdevila. Le gusta conocer a las personas que van a vivir en los espacios que diseña y quiere entender cómo les gustaría vivir. Su principal objetivo es diseñar una casa en la que el cliente esté contento de habitarla. Con sede en Barcelona y una oficina en Mallorca, Pia Capdevila y su equipo se encargan de una amplia gama de proyectos, desde interiores residenciales y comerciales hasta stands de exposiciones, escaparates y eventos especiales.

GANDUXER APARTMENT

BARCELONA, SPAIN

PHOTOS © JORDI CANOSA

The owners of this 180 m^2 apartment requested a complete overhaul of their home, adapting the space to their current needs and allowing as much light as possible to enter their Barcelona residence. With direct sunlight streaming in through the south-facing living area, this space was turned into the main living room with a generous work space. Running the length of the large windows is a custom-built, off-white lacquered desk and long table. The low structure provides a sense of uniformity throughout and which enhances the entry of light. The use of sand-coloured walls and grey strip oak wood flooring also help boost light inside the home.

Les propriétaires de cet appartement de 180 m^2 ont demandé une rénovation complète de leur maison, en adaptant l'espace à leurs besoins actuels et en laissant entrer le plus de lumière possible dans leur résidence de Barcelone. La lumière directe du soleil entrant par l'espace de vie orienté au sud, cet espace est devenu la pièce de vie principale avec un espace de travail généreux. Le long des grandes fenêtres se trouvent un bureau et une longue table laqués blanc cassé fabriqués sur mesure. La structure basse donne un sentiment d'uniformité dans tout l'espace et maximise la lumière. L'utilisation de murs de couleur sable et d'un plancher en bois de chêne avec des bandes grises contribue également à apporter de la lumière à l'intérieur de l'appartement.

Die Eigentümer dieser 180 m^2 großen Wohnung wünschten eine vollständige Renovierung ihres Hauses, um den Raum an ihre aktuellen Bedürfnisse anzupassen und so viel Licht wie möglich in ihre Wohnung in Barcelona zu lassen. Da durch den nach Süden ausgerichteten Wohnbereich direktes Sonnenlicht einfällt, wurde dieser Raum zum Hauptwohnzimmer mit einem großzügigen Arbeitsbereich. An den großen Fenstern stehen ein speziell angefertigter, cremefarben lackierter Schreibtisch und ein langer Tisch. Die niedrige Struktur sorgt für ein Gefühl der Einheitlichkeit im gesamten Raum und maximiert das Licht. Die Verwendung von sandfarbenen Wänden und Eichenholzböden mit grauen Streifen trägt ebenfalls dazu bei, Licht in das Innere der Wohnung zu bringen.

Los propietarios de este apartamento de 180 m^2 solicitaron una reforma completa de su vivienda, adaptando el espacio a sus necesidades actuales y permitiendo la entrada de la mayor cantidad de luz posible en su residencia de Barcelona. Con la luz solar directa que entra por la zona de estar orientada al sur, este espacio se convirtió en la sala de estar principal con un generoso espacio de trabajo. A lo largo de los grandes ventanales hay un escritorio lacado en blanco roto y una mesa larga construidos a medida. La estructura baja proporciona una sensación de uniformidad en todo el espacio y potencia la entrada de luz. El uso de paredes de color arena y el suelo de madera de roble con listones grises también ayudan a potenciar la luz en el interior de la vivienda.

ARIBAU APARTMENT

BARCELONA, SPAIN

PHOTOS © JORDI CANOSA

The brief for the renovation of this large apartment in the elegant Barcelona neighbourhood of the Eixample called for a more spacious day area. On one side of the room, Pia Capdevila opened up the gallery space on one side of the room and turned it into a reading corner connected to the living-dining area. On the other side, the walls of an adjoined room were knocked down to create a work-space integrated with the main living area. A custom-built piece of furniture separating the work area from the living-dining area has a double function: on the dining side, it serves as a stylish sideboard to store crockery and glassware, on the home office side, the cupboards hide all sorts of office material. Book shelves above the desk are designed in the same material as the reading nook and the same light colour palette and different types of wood combined with Herringbone laminate flooring is used throughout.

Der Auftrag für die Renovierung dieser großen Wohnung in Barcelonas elegantem Stadtteil Eixample verlangte einen geräumigeren Tagesbereich. Einerseits öffnete Pia Capdevila den Galerieraum auf einer Seite des Raumes und verwandelte ihn in eine Leseecke, die mit dem Wohn-Esszimmer verbunden ist. Auf der anderen Seite wurden die Wände eines angrenzenden Raumes eingerissen, um einen in den Hauptwohnbereich integrierten Arbeitsbereich zu schaffen. Ein maßgefertigtes Möbelstück, das den Arbeitsbereich vom Wohn-/Esszimmer trennt, hat eine Doppelfunktion: Auf der Seite des Esszimmers dient es als elegantes Sideboard zur Aufbewahrung von Geschirr und Gläsern, auf der Seite des Arbeitsbereichs verbergen Schränke alle Arten von Büroausstattung. Die Regale über dem Schreibtisch sind aus demselben Material wie die Leseecke gestaltet und verwenden dieselbe Palette von hellen Farben und verschiedenen Holzarten in Kombination mit dem Fischgrät-Laminatboden.

La commande de rénovation de ce grand appartement situé dans l'élégant quartier de l'Eixample à Barcelone prévoyait un espace de jour plus spacieux. D'une part, Pia Capdevila a ouvert l'espace de la galerie sur un côté de la pièce et l'a converti en un coin lecture relié au salon-salle à manger. De l'autre côté, les murs d'une pièce adjacente ont été abattus pour créer un espace de travail intégré à l'espace de vie principal. Un meuble sur mesure séparant l'espace de travail du salon/salle à manger a une double fonction : du côté de la salle à manger, il sert d'élégant buffet pour ranger la vaisselle et les verres ; du côté de l'espace de travail, des placards dissimulent toutes sortes d'équipements de bureau. Les étagères au-dessus du bureau sont conçues dans le même matériau que le coin lecture et utilisent la même palette de couleurs claires et de différents types de bois combinés au sol stratifié à chevrons.

El encargo de la reforma de este gran apartamento en el elegante barrio barcelonés del Eixample exigía una zona de día más espaciosa. Por un lado, Pia Capdevila abrió el espacio de la galería de un lado de la habitación y lo convirtió en un rincón de lectura conectado con el salón-comedor. En el otro lado, se derribaron las paredes de una habitación contigua para crear un espacio de trabajo integrado en la zona de estar principal. Un mueble hecho a medida que separa la zona de trabajo del salón-comedor tiene una doble función: en el lado del comedor, sirve de elegante aparador para guardar la vajilla y la cristalería; en el lado de la zona de trabajo, los armarios esconden todo tipo de material de oficina. Las estanterías sobre el escritorio están diseñadas con el mismo material que el rincón de lectura y se utiliza la misma paleta de colores claros y diferentes tipos de madera combinados con el suelo laminado en espiga.

RUST ARCHITECTS

RAANAN STERN, FLORENCIA MICHELLI

www.rustarch com

A young Tel-Aviv based design studio, RUST develops a wide range of architectural and interior design projects from residential, commercial and small office spaces to industrial design and art. In recent years, RUST's projects in the private and business sector have gained esteem. Applying creative solutions to various systems and applications as well as realism, imagination, culture and function, RUST takes on each project as a new and exciting challenge.

RUST ist ein junges Designstudio mit Sitz in Tel Aviv, das eine breite Palette von Architektur- und Innenarchitekturprojekten entwickelt, die von Wohn- und Geschäftsräumen über kleine Büros bis hin zu Industriedesign und Kunst reichen. In den letzten Jahren haben die Projekte von RUST im privaten und geschäftlichen Bereich an Wertschätzung gewonnen. Durch die Anwendung kreativer Lösungen für verschiedene Systeme und Anwendungen sowie Realismus, Vorstellungskraft, Kultur und Funktion nimmt RUST jedes Projekt als neue und spannende Herausforderung an.

WORK AND LIVE APARTMENT

Jeune studio de design basé à Tel-Aviv, RUST développe une large gamme de projets d'architecture et de design d'intérieur, allant des espaces résidentiels, commerciaux et de petits bureaux au design industriel et à l'art. Ces dernières années, les projets de RUST dans le secteur privé et commercial ont gagné en estime. En appliquant des solutions créatives à divers systèmes et applications ainsi que le réalisme, l'imagination, la culture et la fonction, RUST aborde chaque projet comme un nouveau défi passionnant.

RUST, un joven estudio de diseño con sede en Tel-Aviv, desarrolla una amplia gama de proyectos de arquitectura y diseño de interiores, desde espacios residenciales, comerciales y pequeñas oficinas hasta diseño industrial y arte. En los últimos años, los proyectos de RUST en el sector privado y empresarial han ganado en estima. Aplicando soluciones creativas a diversos sistemas y aplicaciones, así como realismo, imaginación, cultura y función, RUST asume cada proyecto como un nuevo y emocionante reto.

WORK AND LIVE APARTMENT

TEL AVIV, ISRAEL

PHOTOS © YOAV PELED

The young couple living in this small apartment needed a living space that could sit comfortably alongside a working space, without sacrificing intimacy and maintaining a clear separation between all activities. Characterized by high ceilings and strip windows, RUST carved out a comfortable workspace in the middle of this 57 m^2 apartment with clearly defined private and public areas. A glass box with iron frames further separates the day area from the night area and neatly contains two work stations. Double-layered wooden floors, insulated walls, exposed brick and acoustic ceiling tiles in the office space facilitate the parallel use of different functions throughout this home.

Das junge Paar, das in dieser kleinen Wohnung lebt, benötigte einen Wohnraum, der bequem neben einem Arbeitsbereich Platz findet, ohne dass die Intimität verloren geht und eine klare Trennung zwischen allen Aktivitäten aufrechterhalten wird. Mit hohen Decken und Fensterbändern schuf RUST in der Mitte der 57 m^2 großen Wohnung einen komfortablen Arbeitsbereich mit klar definierten privaten und öffentlichen Bereichen. Ein Glaskasten mit Eisenrahmen trennt den Tagesbereich vom Nachtbereich und enthält zwei Arbeitsplätze. Zweischichtige Holzböden, isolierte Wände, Sichtziegel und Akustikdeckenplatten im Büroraum erleichtern die parallele Nutzung der verschiedenen Funktionen in dieser Wohnung.

Le jeune couple vivant dans ce petit appartement avait besoin d'un espace de vie qui puisse s'installer confortablement à côté d'un espace de travail, sans sacrifier l'intimité et en maintenant une séparation claire entre toutes les activités. Caractérisé par de hauts plafonds et des fenêtres à bandes, RUST a sculpté un espace de travail confortable au milieu de cet appartement de 57 m^2 avec des zones privées et publiques clairement définies. Une boîte en verre avec des cadres en fer sépare encore plus la zone de jour de la zone de nuit et contient deux postes de travail. Des sols en bois à double couche, des murs isolés, des briques apparentes et des dalles acoustiques au plafond dans l'espace bureau facilitent l'utilisation parallèle de différentes fonctions dans toute la maison.

La joven pareja que vivía en este pequeño apartamento necesitaba un espacio de vida que pudiera convivir cómodamente con un espacio de trabajo, sin sacrificar la intimidad y manteniendo una clara separación entre todas las actividades. Caracterizado por techos altos y ventanas en forma de tira, RUST creó un cómodo espacio de trabajo en el centro de este apartamento de 57 m^2 con zonas privadas y públicas claramente definidas. Una caja de cristal con marcos de hierro separa aún más la zona de día de la de noche y contiene ordenadamente dos puestos de trabajo. Los suelos de madera de doble capa, las paredes aisladas, el ladrillo visto y las baldosas acústicas del techo en el espacio de oficina facilitan el uso paralelo de diferentes funciones en toda esta vivienda.

DAY
100

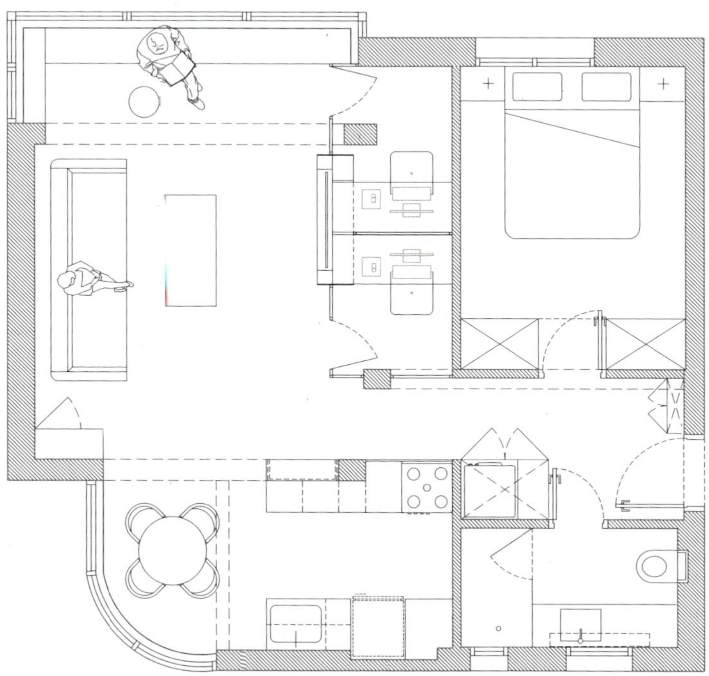

Floor plan

SARAH BARNARD

SARAH BARNARD

www.sarahbarnard.com

A WELL and LEED-accredited designer, Sarah Barnard was recognized as a "Ones to Watch" Scholar by the American Society of Interior Designers (ASID) in 2017. Sarah designs environments that support mental, physical and emotional wellbeing and creates highly personalized, restorative spaces that are deeply connected to art and the preservation of the environment. She is an advocate for a conscious, inclusive and compassionate creative design process.

Sarah Barnard ist eine WELL- und LEED-zertifizierte Designerin und wurde 2017 von der American Society of Interior Designers (ASID) als „Ones to Watch"-Stipendiatin ausgezeichnet. Sarah Barnard entwirft Umgebungen, die das geistige, körperliche und emotionale Wohlbefinden unterstützen, und schafft hochgradig personalisierte, erholsame Räume, die eng mit der Kunst und der Erhaltung der Umwelt verbunden sind. Sie ist eine Verfechterin eines bewussten, integrativen und mitfühlenden kreativen Designprozesses.

BEAMING BIBLIOPHILE

OCEANVIEW PENTHOUSE

Designer accréditée WELL et LEED, Sarah Barnard a été reconnue comme une boursière « Ones to Watch » par la Société américaine des designers d'intérieur (ASID) en 2017. Sarah conçoit des environnements qui favorisent le bien-être mental, physique et émotionnel et crée des espaces hautement personnalisés et réparateurs, profondément liés à l'art et à la préservation de l'environnement. Elle est un défenseur d'un processus de conception créative conscient, inclusif et compatissant.

Diseñadora acreditada por WELL y LEED, Sarah Barnard fue reconocida como becaria «Ones to Watch» por la Sociedad Americana de Diseñadores de Interiores (ASID) en 2017. Sarah diseña entornos que apoyan el bienestar mental, físico y emocional y crea espacios altamente personalizados y restauradores que están profundamente conectados con el arte y la preservación del medio ambiente. Es una defensora de un proceso de diseño creativo consciente, inclusivo y compasivo.

BEAMING BIBLIOPHILE

LOS ANGELES, CALIFORNIA, UNITED STATES

PHOTOS © STEVEN DEWALL

This nature-inspired contemporary office features a neutral and earth-toned palette and agate-inspired grasscloth wallpaper. A fiddle leaf fig, air plant and agave add greenery, connecting the outside with thee inside space. A desk in black powder-coated steel was built to fit the homeowner's specific needs and is complemented with an ergonomic chair. Dark curtains create a calm atmosphere for more introspective work or for a moment's rest in the hectic day. A sleek sofa adds a warm touch and offers a place to repose or a comfortable setting to read or review items away from the computer space. A pillow embroidered with Picasso illustrations give an idea of the homeowner's creative interests, while a custom bookshelf provides ample space for books and artwork.

Dieses von der Natur inspirierte zeitgenössische Büro zeichnet sich durch eine neutrale und erdfarbene Farbpalette und eine von Achat inspirierte Grasfasertapete aus. Eine Fiddle-Leaf-Feige, eine Luftpflanze und eine Agave sorgen für Grün und verbinden den Außenbereich mit dem Innenbereich. Ein Schreibtisch aus schwarzem, pulverbeschichtetem Stahl wurde speziell für die Bedürfnisse des Hausbesitzers angefertigt und durch einen ergonomischen Stuhl ergänzt. Dunkle Vorhänge schaffen eine ruhige Atmosphäre für konzentriertes Arbeiten oder für einen Moment der Ruhe im hektischen Alltag. Ein elegantes Sofa verleiht dem Raum eine warme Note und bietet einen Platz zum Ausruhen oder eine bequeme Umgebung, um abseits des Computers zu lesen oder Dinge zu überprüfen. Ein mit Picasso-Illustrationen besticktes Kissen vermittelt einen Eindruck von den kreativen Interessen des Hausbesitzers, während ein maßgefertigtes Bücherregal reichlich Platz für Bücher und Kunstwerke bietet.

Ce bureau contemporain inspiré par la nature présente une palette de couleurs neutres et terreuses et un papier peint en toile de gazon inspiré de l'agate. Un figuier à feuilles de violon, une plante aérienne et un agave ajoutent de la verdure, reliant l'extérieur à l'intérieur de l'espace. Un bureau en acier noir revêtu de poudre a été construit pour répondre aux besoins spécifiques du propriétaire et est complété par une chaise ergonomique. Des rideaux sombres créent une atmosphère calme pour un travail plus introspectif ou pour un moment de repos dans une journee trépidante. Un canapé élégant ajoute une touche chaleureuse et offre un endroit pour se reposer ou un cadre confortable pour lire ou revoir des articles loin de l'espace informatique. Un coussin brodé d'illustrations de Picasso donne une idée des intérêts créatifs du propriétaire, tandis qu'une étagère personnalisée offre un grand espace pour les livres et les œuvres d'art.

Esta oficina contemporánea inspirada en la naturaleza presenta una paleta de tonos neutros y tierra y un papel pintado de tela de hierba inspirado en el ágata. Una higuera de hoja de violín, una planta de aire y un agave añaden vegetación, conectando el exterior con el espacio interior. Un escritorio de acero con recubrimiento de polvo negro se construyó para adaptarse a las necesidades específicas del propietario y se complementa con una silla ergonómica. Las cortinas oscuras crean un ambiente tranquilo para el trabajo más introspectivo o para un momento de descanso en la agitada jornada. Un elegante sofá añade un toque cálido y ofrece un lugar de reposo o un entorno cómodo para leer o revisar artículos lejos del espacio del ordenador. Un cojín bordado con ilustraciones de Picasso da una idea de los intereses creativos del propietario, mientras que una estantería a medida ofrece un amplio espacio para libros y obras de arte.

OCEANVIEW PENTHOUSE

LOS ANGELES, CALIFORNIA, UNITED STATES

PHOTOS © STEVEN DEWALL

A deep custom sofa in wool felt is the focus point of this creative workspace with sweeping ocean views. Large enough to work, nap, daydream or socialize, the sofa sits behind a wide floating desk by Hobstetter Architecture Studio paired with a sleek chair designed by Mauro Lipparini. The chair neatly tucks into the desk, thus offering minimal interruption to the spectacular views. The sofa is flanked by side tables made of natural maple and steel. Subtle decorative elements throughout the office space contribute to the overall view and sense of calm, such a "Cumulous" a fibre sculpture by Renae Barnard. This woven sculpture was made from wire, thread, yarn, rope, lamp cord, and an assortment of new and recycled materials commissioned to celebrate the natural environment.

Ein tiefes, maßgefertigtes Sofa aus Wollfilz ist der Mittelpunkt dieses kreativen Arbeitsbereichs mit weitem Meerblick. Das Sofa ist groß genug, um zu arbeiten, ein Nickerchen zu machen, zu träumen oder Kontakte zu knüpfen. Es befindet sich hinter einem breiten, schwebenden Schreibtisch von Hobstetter Architecture Studio, der mit einem eleganten Stuhl von Mauro Lipparini kombiniert wurde. Der Stuhl fügt sich nahtlos in den Schreibtisch ein, so dass die spektakuläre Aussicht nur minimal beeinträchtigt wird. Das Sofa wird von Beistelltischen aus natürlichem Ahornholz und Stahl flankiert. Subtile dekorative Elemente im gesamten Büroraum tragen zum Gesamtbild und zum Gefühl der Ruhe bei, wie zum Beispiel „Cumulous", eine Faserskulptur von Renae Barnard. Diese gewebte Skulptur wurde aus Draht, Faden, Garn, Seil, Lampenschnur und einer Auswahl neuer und recycelter Materialien hergestellt, die in Auftrag gegeben wurden, um die natürliche Umgebung zu feiern.

Un profond canapé personnalisé en feutre de laine est le point central de cet espace de travail créatif avec vue imprenable sur l'océan. Suffisamment grand pour travailler, faire la sieste, rêvasser ou rencontrer des gens, le canapé se trouve derrière un large bureau flottant créé par Hobstetter Architecture Studio, associé à une chaise élégante conçue par Mauro Lipparini. La chaise s'intègre parfaitement au bureau, offrant ainsi une interruption minimale des vues spectaculaires. Le canapé est flanqué de tables d'appoint en érable naturel et en acier. De subtils éléments décoratifs répartis dans tout l'espace de bureau contribuent à la vue d'ensemble et au sentiment de calme, comme « Cumulous », une sculpture en fibre de Renae Barnard. Cette sculpture tissée a été réalisée à partir de fils métalliques, de fils, de cordes, de cordons de lampes et d'un assortiment de matériaux neufs et recyclés commandés pour célébrer l'environnement naturel.

Un profundo sofá de fieltro de lana es el centro de atención de este espacio de trabajo creativo con amplias vistas al océano. Lo suficientemente grande como para trabajar, dormir la siesta, soñar o socializar, el sofá se sitúa detrás de un amplio escritorio flotante del estudio de arquitectura Hobstetter, que se combina con una elegante silla diseñada por Mauro Lipparini. La silla queda perfectamente integrada en el escritorio, lo que supone una interrupción mínima de las espectaculares vistas. El sofá está flanqueado por mesas auxiliares de arce natural y acero. Sutiles elementos decorativos en todo el espacio de la oficina contribuyen a la vista general y a la sensación de calma, como «Cumulous», una escultura de fibra de Renae Barnard. Esta escultura tejida está hecha con alambre, hilo, cuerda, cordón de lámpara y un surtido de materiales nuevos y reciclados encargados para celebrar el entorno natural.

SHIRA LAVI

SHIRA LAVI

www.shiralavi.com

Specialised in architecture and interior design of living and working spaces, Shira Lavi creates fundamentally minimalist spaces focused on spatial order and geometric proportions. Shira Lavi's personal projects are unique and aim to make the user's lives easier, more pleasant and filled with positive energy. Avoiding fast-moving design trends, Shira Lavi aims to design high-quality practical designs with a focus on the specific needs of each client. Each project is planned to the finest detail and starts with the examination of the client's needs, habits, desires and dreams, as well as the analysis of the structure, environment and unique history of the place that will be inhabited.

Shira Lavi hat sich auf Architektur und Innenarchitektur von Wohn- und Arbeitsräumen spezialisiert. Sie schafft grundsätzlich minimalistische Räume mit dem Schwerpunkt auf räumlicher Ordnung und geometrischen Proportionen. Die persönlichen Projekte von Shira Lavi sind einzigartig und zielen darauf ab, das Leben der Nutzer einfacher, angenehmer und voller positiver Energie zu gestalten. Shira Lavi vermeidet schnell wechselnde Designtrends und ist bestrebt, qualitativ hochwertige, praktische Designs zu entwerfen, die sich auf die spezifischen Bedürfnisse jedes einzelnen Kunden konzentrieren. Jedes Projekt wird bis ins kleinste Detail geplant und beginnt mit einer Untersuchung der Bedürfnisse, Gewohnheiten, Wünsche und Träume des Kunden sowie mit einer Analyse der Struktur, der Umgebung und der einzigartigen Geschichte des zu bewohnenden Ortes.

HOUSE OF LOVE

URBAN ZEN HOUSE

Spécialisée dans l'architecture et la décoration intérieure des espaces de vie et de travail, Shira Lavi crée des espaces fondamentalement minimalistes en mettant l'accent sur l'ordre spatial et les proportions géométriques. Les projets personnels de Shira Lavi sont uniques et visent à rendre la vie de l'utilisateur plus facile, plus agréable et pleine d'énergie positive. Évitant les tendances de conception qui changent rapidement, Shira Lavi vise à produire des conceptions pratiques de haute qualité, axées sur les besoins spécifiques de chaque client. Chaque projet est planifié dans les moindres détails et commence par un examen des besoins, des habitudes, des désirs et des rêves du client, ainsi que par une analyse de la structure, de l'environnement et de l'histoire unique du lieu à habiter.

Especializada en arquitectura y diseño de interiores de espacios de vida y trabajo, Shira Lavi crea espacios fundamentalmente minimalistas centrados en el orden espacial y las proporciones geométricas. Los proyectos personales de Shira Lavi son únicos y pretenden hacer la vida del usuario más fácil, agradable y llena de energía positiva. Evitando las tendencias de diseño que cambian rápidamente, Shira Lavi se propone realizar diseños prácticos de alta calidad centrados en las necesidades específicas de cada cliente. Cada proyecto se planifica hasta el más mínimo detalle y comienza con el examen de las necesidades, los hábitos, los deseos y los sueños del cliente, así como con el análisis de la estructura, el entorno y la historia única del lugar que se va a habitar.

HOUSE OF LOVE

RAMAT HASHARON, ISRAEL

PHOTOS © SHAI GIL

Situated in a row of four attached houses built in the 1970s, Shira Lavi set about freeing this "caged box" by opening it up to give it a sense of space and height. Opening the interior as much as possible was key to accommodate the needs of a family of seven (two parents and five children) and to create a fluid, open, well-lit and ventilated home. An expansive library made from coloured MDF plates stretches from the ground floor up to the ceiling of the upstairs level and contains the family's extensive book collection, as well as drawers for storage, a closet and a drinks cabinet. A new rooftop level was created to house the master suite, separated from the rest of the house. Making the most of the modest space, storage units and a small home office were design around the suite, seamlessly integrated into this minimalist space.

In einer Reihe von vier Reihenhäusern aus den 1970er Jahren gelegen, wollte Shira Lavi diesen „Käfig" befreien, indem sie ihn öffnete, um ihm ein Gefühl von Raum und Höhe zu geben. Die größtmögliche Öffnung des Innenraums war der Schlüssel, um die Bedürfnisse einer siebenköpfigen Familie (zwei Eltern und fünf Kinder) zu erfüllen und eine fließende, offene, helle und luftige Wohnung zu schaffen. Eine geräumige Bibliothek aus farbigen MDF-Platten erstreckt sich vom Erdgeschoss bis zur Decke des Obergeschosses und beherbergt die umfangreiche Büchersammlung der Familie sowie Schubladen zur Aufbewahrung, einen Schrank und einen Getränkeschrank. Für die Master-Suite wurde ein neues Dachgeschoss geschaffen, das vom Rest des Hauses getrennt ist. Unter Ausnutzung des bescheidenen Platzes wurden um die Suite herum Stauräume und ein kleines Home-Office eingerichtet, die sich nahtlos in diesen minimalistischen Raum einfügen.

Située dans une rangée de quatre maisons mitoyennes construites dans les années 1970, Shira Lavi a entrepris de libérer cette « boîte en cage » en l'ouvrant pour lui donner un sentiment d'espace et de hauteur. Ouvrir l'intérieur autant que possible était essentiel pour répondre aux besoins d'une famille de sept personnes (deux parents et cinq enfants) et pour créer une maison fluide, ouverte, bien éclairée et ventilée. Une vaste bibliothèque faite de plaques de MDF colorées s'étend du rez-de-chaussée jusqu'au plafond de l'étage et contient la vaste collection de livres de la famille, ainsi que des tiroirs de rangement, une armoire et un meuble à boissons. Un nouveau niveau sur le toit a été créé pour abriter la suite parentale, séparée du reste de la maison. Pour tirer le meilleur parti de cet espace modeste, des unités de rangement et un petit bureau à domicile ont été conçus autour de la suite, s'intégrant parfaitement à cet espace minimaliste.

Situada en una hilera de cuatro casas adosadas construidas en los años 70, Shira Lavi se propuso liberar esta «caja enjaulada» abriéndola para darle una sensación de espacio y altura. Abrir el interior al máximo era la clave para acomodar las necesidades de una familia de siete miembros (dos padres y cinco hijos) y crear una vivienda fluida, abierta, bien iluminada y ventilada. Una amplia biblioteca hecha con placas de MDF de colores se extiende desde la planta baja hasta el techo del nivel superior y contiene la extensa colección de libros de la familia, así como cajones para el almacenamiento, un armario y un mueble de bebidas. Se creó un nuevo nivel en la azotea para albergar la suite principal, separada del resto de la casa. Aprovechando el modesto espacio, se diseñaron unidades de almacenamiento y una pequeña oficina en casa alrededor de la suite, integradas a la perfección en este espacio minimalista.

Section

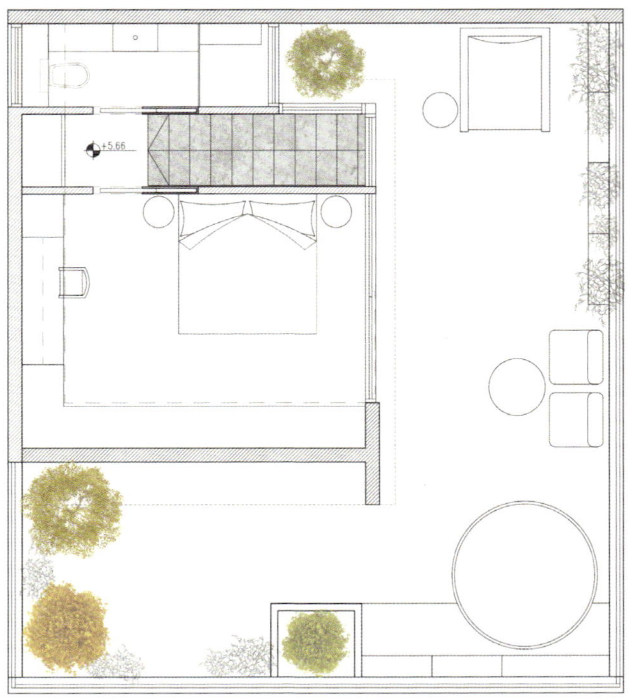

Floor plan

URBAN ZEN HOUSE

TEL AVIV, ISRAEL

PHOTOS © SHAI GIL

Located in a northern neighbourhood of Tel Aviv, this four-story urban home with minimalist interior is a quiet refuge from the bustling city. Each family member has their own private space and quality family time and social gatherings are held in the ground floor communal area dominated by a wooden oak grid. The main structure on the ground floor acts as a partition, a door, a shelf and a kitchen cabinet. The main partition is thin with a glass element and functions as a closet for coats, office storage and a television console. It also features a full-height glass door, which acts as an entrance to the home office and separation from the living room. The central wooden theme continues in to the spacious, yet intimate, home office, which is big enough for two people to work at the same time. The same minimalist colour and texture palette used throughout the home can be found in the office, creating a thread of continuity and offering a peaceful environment.

Dieses vierstöckige Stadthaus mit minimalistischem Interieur liegt in einem nördlichen Viertel von Tel Aviv und ist ein ruhiger Rückzugsort von der hektischen Stadt. Jedes Familienmitglied hat seinen eigenen privaten Bereich, während der Gemeinschaftsbereich im Erdgeschoss, der von einem Eichenholzgitter dominiert wird, als Treffpunkt für die Familie genutzt wird. Die Hauptstruktur im Erdgeschoss dient als Trennwand, Tür, Regal und Küchenschrank. Die Haupttrennwand ist dünn und mit einem Glaselement versehen und dient als Garderobenschrank, Büroablage und TV-Konsole. Es hat auch eine raumhohe Glastür, die als Eingang zum Büro und als Abgrenzung zum Wohnzimmer dient. Das zentrale Holzthema setzt sich in den geräumigen und doch intimen Büroräumen fort, die groß genug sind, dass zwei Personen gleichzeitig arbeiten können. Die gleiche minimalistische Farbpalette und Textur, die im gesamten Haus verwendet wird, findet sich auch im Büro wieder, wodurch ein roter Faden entsteht und eine ruhige Umgebung geschaffen wird.

Située dans un quartier du nord de Tel Aviv, cette maison de ville de quatre étages à l'intérieur minimaliste est un refuge tranquille loin de la ville animée. Chaque membre de la famille dispose de son propre espace privé, tandis que les moments de qualité en famille et les réunions sociales se déroulent dans l'espace commun du rez-de-chaussée, dominé par un treillis en chêne. La structure principale du rez-de-chaussée sert de cloison, de porte, d'étagère et de placard de cuisine. La cloison principale est mince avec un élément en verre et fait office de placard à vêtements, de rangement de bureau et de console de télévision. Il dispose également d'une porte vitrée pleine hauteur, qui sert d'entrée au bureau et de séparation avec le salon. Le thème central du bois se poursuit dans l'espace de bureau à la fois spacieux et intime, qui est suffisamment grand pour que deux personnes puissent y travailler en même temps. La même palette de couleurs et de textures minimalistes utilisée dans toute la maison se retrouve dans le bureau, créant un fil conducteur et offrant une atmosphère tranquille.

Situada en un barrio del norte de Tel Aviv, esta casa urbana de cuatro plantas con un interior minimalista es un tranquilo refugio de la bulliciosa ciudad. Cada miembro de la familia tiene su propio espacio privado y el tiempo familiar de calidad y las reuniones sociales se celebran en la zona común de la planta baja, dominada por una rejilla de madera de roble. La estructura principal de la planta baja hace las veces de tabique, puerta, estantería y armario de cocina. El tabique principal es delgado con un elemento de cristal y funciona como armario para los abrigos, almacén de oficina y consola de televisión. También cuenta con una puerta de cristal a toda altura, que sirve de entrada al despacho y de separación del salón. El tema central de la madera continúa en el espacioso, pero íntimo, espacio de oficina, que es lo suficientemente grande para que dos personas trabajen al mismo tiempo. La misma paleta de colores y texturas minimalistas utilizada en toda la casa se puede encontrar en la oficina, creando un hilo de continuidad y ofreciendo un ambiente tranquilo.

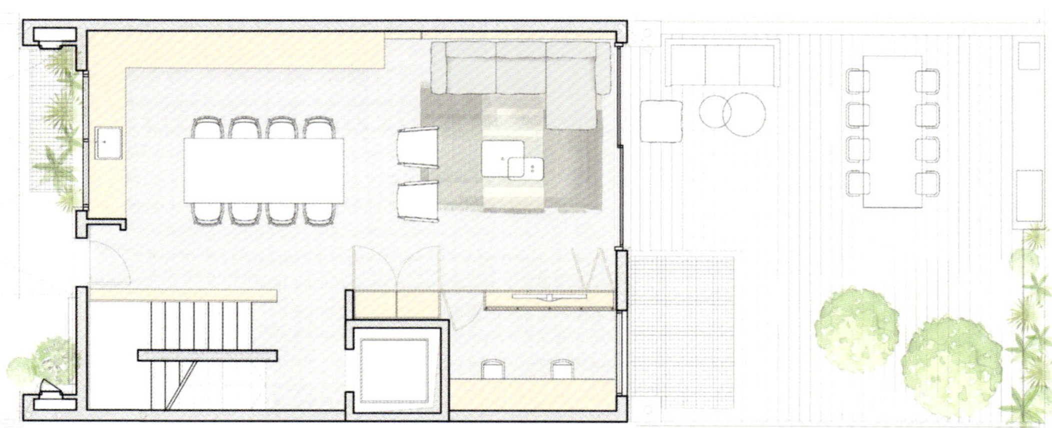

Floor plan

SILVIA ALLORI

SILVIA ALLORI

www.silviaallori.it

Passionate about interior design, Silvia Allori applies a multidisciplinary approach to her design, which allows her to create for a wide range of disciplines, from interior design to fashion branding. Silvia lives and works between Milan and Florence, and since 2016, she has been part of the set design and events production studio, Archivio Personal.

Als leidenschaftliche Innenarchitektin wendet Silvia Allori einen multidisziplinären Ansatz für ihr Design an, der es ihr ermöglicht, für eine breite Palette von Disziplinen zu entwerfen, von der Innenarchitektur bis hin zum Branding von Mode. Silvia lebt und arbeitet zwischen Mailand und Florenz. Seit 2016 ist sie Teil des Studios für Szenografie und Eventproduktion Archivio Personal.

SILVIA'S HOME & OFFICE

Passionnée par l'architecture d'intérieur, Silvia Allori applique une approche multidisciplinaire à son design, ce qui lui permet de créer pour un large éventail de disciplines, de la décoration d'intérieur à l'image de marque de la mode. Silvia vit et travaille entre Milan et Florence, et depuis 2016, elle fait partie du studio de scénographie et de production d'événements Archivio Personal.

Apasionada del diseño de interiores, Silvia Allori aplica un enfoque multidisciplinar a su diseño, lo que le permite crear para una amplia gama de disciplinas, desde el diseño de interiores hasta la creación de marcas de moda. Silvia vive y trabaja entre Milán y Florencia, y desde 2016 forma parte del estudio de escenografía y producción de eventos Archivio Personal.

SILVIA'S HOME & OFFICE

FLORENCE, ITALY

PHOTOS © SIMONE BOSSI

Silvia Allori immediately fell in love with the 46 m^2 apartment designed by 1970s Italian architect and furniture design Roberto Monsani. Silvia completely renovated the space and turned it into her own smart and functional home and office. The predominant white laminate hides cabinets, a table, neon lights and plasters. Disappearing into white laminated niches are cabinets and a table, neon lights filter through holes in the wall and cladding and slender rectangular bars serving as an entrance guide to the home. The main space can be filled or emptied with a sofa, bed and table. Storage and display can be created by slotting bookshelves and pegs into holes in the walls and a gold metallic curtain separating the kitchen work surface from the corridor helps create a clutter-free space. Neutral colours and wood flooring throughout give the interior of this tiny home a soft and cosy atmosphere.

Silvia Allori verliebte sich sofort in die 46 m^2 große Wohnung, die vom italienischen Architekten und Möbeldesigner Roberto Monsani in den 1970er Jahren entworfen wurde. Silvia hat den Raum komplett renoviert und in ihr eigenes schickes und funktionales Zuhause und Büro verwandelt. Hinter dem vorherrschenden weißen Laminat verbergen sich Schränke, ein Tisch, Neonröhren und Gipsabdrücke. In Nischen aus weißem Laminat verschwinden Schränke und ein Tisch, Neonlichter, die durch Löcher in der Wand und in der Vertäfelung dringen, sowie schmale, rechteckige Stangen, die als Einstieg in den Wohnbereich dienen. Der Hauptraum kann mit einem Sofa, einem Bett und einem Tisch gefüllt oder geleert werden. In den Löchern in den Wänden können Regale und Kleiderbügel angebracht werden, und ein goldener Metallvorhang, der die Arbeitsfläche der Küche vom Flur trennt, sorgt für einen aufgeräumten Raum. Neutrale Farben und Holzböden verleihen dem Inneren dieses kleinen Hauses eine weiche und gemütliche Atmosphäre.

Silvia Allori est immédiatement tombée amoureuse de l'appartement de 46 m^2 conçu par Roberto Monsani, architecte et designer de meubles italien des années 1970. Silvia a entièrement rénové l'espace et l'a transformé en une maison et un bureau intelligents et fonctionnels. Le stratifié blanc prédominant cache des armoires, une table, des néons et des moulages en plâtre. Dans des niches de stratifié blanc disparaissent des armoires et une table, des néons qui filtrent à travers des trous dans le mur et des lambris et des barres rectangulaires élancées qui servent de guides d'entrée dans l'espace de vie. L'espace principal peut être rempli ou vidé avec un canapé, un lit et une table. Il est possible de créer des espaces de rangement et de présentation en glissant des étagères et des cintres dans les trous des murs, et un rideau métallique doré séparant le plan de travail de la cuisine du couloir permet de créer un espace sans encombrement. Les couleurs neutres et le parquet en bois confèrent à l'intérieur de cette petite maison une atmosphère douce et confortable.

Silvia Allori se enamoró inmediatamente del apartamento de 46 m^2 diseñado por el arquitecto y diseñador de muebles italiano de los años 70 Roberto Monsani. Silvia renovó por completo el espacio y lo convirtió en su propia casa y oficina inteligente y funcional. El laminado blanco predominante esconde armarios, una mesa, luces de neón y yesos. Desapareciendo en nichos de laminado blanco hay armarios y una mesa, luces de neón que se filtran a través de agujeros en la pared y revestimientos y esbeltas barras rectangulares que sirven de guía de entrada a la vivienda. El espacio principal puede llenarse o vaciarse con un sofá, una cama y una mesa. El almacenamiento y la exposición pueden crearse encajando estanterías y perchas en los agujeros de las paredes, y una cortina metálica dorada que separa la superficie de trabajo de la cocina del pasillo ayuda a crear un espacio libre de desorden. Los colores neutros y el suelo de madera dan al interior de esta pequeña casa un ambiente suave y acogedor.

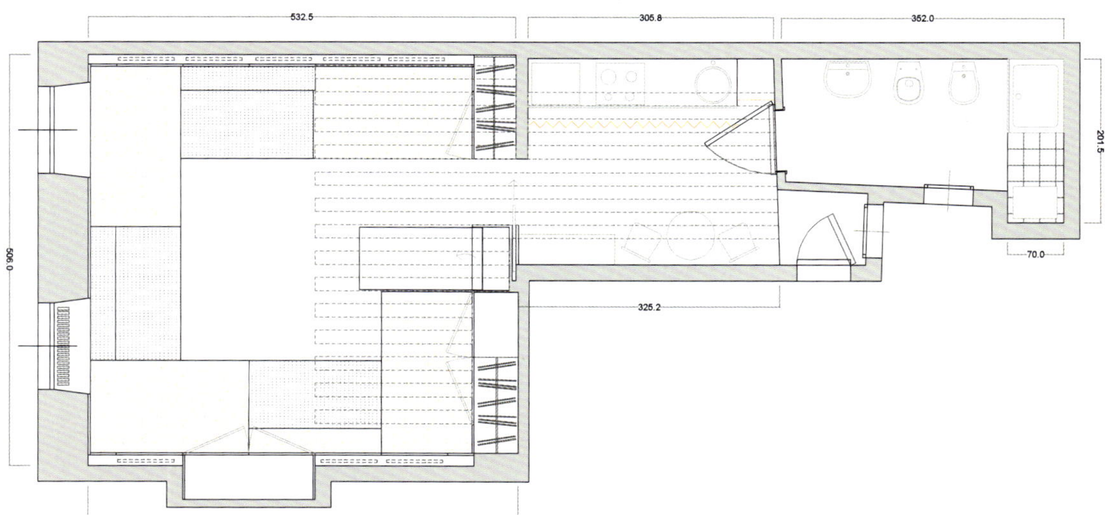

Floor plan

SOL HAUS DESIGN

VINA LUTADO

www.solhausdesign.com

With an architecture degree from the University of South California, Vina Lutado spent two decades working in high-end corporate architecture for notable firms in Los Angeles, San Francisco and Chicago. In 2002, however, after completing an international fellowship in Germany, Vina committed herself to ecologically-sound and affordable building practices. Her California-based design firm, Sol Haus Design, focuses on small-scale projects which make a positive difference. She has a simple and effective approach to design, which promotes a sustainable lifestyle that goes beyond the confines of the home or office. Vina manifested her dream of living simply and with a minimum ecological footprint when she completed her own house, the 140-square-foot Tiny House.

Nach ihrem Abschluss in Architektur an der University of Southern California arbeitete Vina Lutado zwei Jahrzehnte lang in namhaften Unternehmen in Los Angeles, San Francisco und Chicago im Bereich der hochwertigen Unternehmensarchitektur. Doch 2002, nach einem internationalen Stipendium in Deutschland, engagierte sich Vina für umweltfreundliche und erschwingliche Baupraktiken. Ihr in Kalifornien ansässiges Designbüro, Sol Haus Design, konzentriert sich auf kleine Projekte, die einen positiven Beitrag leisten. Sie verfolgt einen einfachen und effektiven Designansatz, der einen nachhaltigen Lebensstil über die Grenzen von Wohnung und Büro hinaus fördert. Vina verwirklichte ihren Traum vom einfachen Leben mit einem minimalen ökologischen Fußabdruck, als sie ihr eigenes Haus, das 14 m^2 große Tiny House, fertig stellte.

VINA'S TINY HOUSE

Diplômée en architecture de l'université de Californie du Sud, Vina Lutado a travaillé pendant vingt ans dans le domaine de l'architecture d'entreprise haut de gamme pour des cabinets renommés de Los Angeles, San Francisco et Chicago. Toutefois, en 2002, après avoir obtenu une bourse internationale en Allemagne, Vina s'est engagée dans des pratiques de construction écologiques et abordables. Sa société de design basée en Californie, Sol Haus Design, se concentre sur des projets à petite échelle qui font une différence positive. Elle adopte une approche simple et efficace du design qui favorise un mode de vie durable au-delà des limites de la maison ou du bureau. Vina a réalisé son rêve de vivre simplement et avec une empreinte écologique minimale en achevant sa propre maison, la Tiny House de 14 m^2.

Licenciada en arquitectura por la Universidad de California del Sur, Vina Lutado pasó dos décadas trabajando en arquitectura corporativa de alto nivel para notables firmas de Los Ángeles, San Francisco y Chicago. Sin embargo, en 2002, tras completar una beca internacional en Alemania, Vina se comprometió con prácticas de construcción ecológicas y asequibles. Su empresa de diseño con sede en California, Sol Haus Design, se centra en proyectos a pequeña escala que marcan una diferencia positiva. Tiene un enfoque sencillo y eficaz del diseño, que promueve un estilo de vida sostenible yendo más allá de los límites del hogar o la oficina. Vina hizo realidad su sueño de vivir de forma sencilla y con una huella ecológica mínima cuando completó su propia casa, la Tiny House de 14 m^2.

VINA'S TINY HOUSE

OJAI, CAIFORNIA, UNITED STATES

PHOTOS © EILEEN RINGWALD AND CHIBI MOKU

Embracing the 'less is more' principle, Vina set out to build herself a house that reflects her core values of simplicity, sustainability and living within one's means. Her off-the-grid home took 13 months to complete (with the help of local artists and craftsmen in Ojai, California) and cost $35,000. It is based on an 8 by 20-foot trailer and offers 14 m² of interior living space. Using solar panels and passive heating and cooling techniques, the Tiny House is completely self-sufficient. The timeless interior is finished with non-toxic materials and it is equipped with a gas fireplace and operable skylights. In spite its size, the interior of this house feels spacious and is bathed in natural light and has room for a generous work space, which has been carved out of the window in the main living space. It is designed with lots of storage space and multi-purpose and moveable furniture to maximize functionality.

Nach dem Prinzip „weniger ist mehr" wollte Vina ein Haus bauen, das ihre zentralen Werte wie Einfachheit, Nachhaltigkeit und ein Leben im Rahmen ihrer Möglichkeiten widerspiegelt. Die Fertigstellung ihres netzunabhängigen Hauses dauerte 13 Monate (mit Hilfe örtlicher Künstler und Handwerker in Ojai, Kalifornien) und kostete 35.000 Dollar. Er basiert auf einem 2,40 x 6 m großen Anhänger und bietet 14 m² Innenfläche. Durch den Einsatz von Sonnenkollektoren und passiven Heiz- und Kühltechniken ist das Tiny House völlig autark. Der zeitlose Innenraum ist mit ungiftigen Materialien ausgestattet und verfügt über einen Gaskamin und bedienbare Oberlichter. Trotz seiner Größe wirkt das Innere des Hauses geräumig, ist lichtdurchflutet und bietet Platz für einen großzügigen Arbeitsbereich, der aus dem Fenster des Hauptwohnzimmers herausgeschnitten wurde. Das Haus bietet viel Stauraum und vielseitig einsetzbare, bewegliche Möbel, um die Funktionalität und Wohnlichkeit zu maximieren.

Adoptant le principe du « moins, c'est plus », Vina a entrepris de se construire une maison qui reflète ses valeurs fondamentales de simplicité, de durabilité et de respect de ses moyens. La construction de sa maison hors réseau a duré 13 mois (avec l'aide d'artistes et d'artisans locaux à Ojai, en Californie) et a coûté 35 000 dollars. Il est basé sur une remorque de 2,40 x par 6 m et offre 14 m² d'espace intérieur. Grâce à l'utilisation de panneaux solaires et de techniques de chauffage et de refroidissement passifs, la Tiny House est totalement autosuffisante. L'intérieur intemporel est fini avec des matériaux non toxiques et est équipé d'une cheminée à gaz et de lucarnes ouvrantes. Malgré sa taille, l'intérieur de cette maison est spacieux, baigné de lumière naturelle et dispose d'un espace de travail généreux, qui a été découpé dans la fenêtre de l'espace de vie principal. La maison offre de nombreux espaces de rangement et des meubles polyvalents et mobiles pour maximiser la fonctionnalité et l'habitabilité.

Adoptando el principio de «menos es más», Vina propuso construirse una casa que reflejara sus valores fundamentales de simplicidad, sostenibilidad y vida dentro de sus posibilidades. Su casa sin conexión a la red tardó 13 meses en completarse (con la ayuda de artistas y artesanos locales de Ojai, California) y costó 35.000 dólares. Se basa en un remolque de 2.40 x por 6 m. y ofrece 14 m² de espacio interior. Utilizando paneles solares y técnicas de calefacción y refrigeración pasivas, la Tiny House es completamente autosuficiente. El interior atemporal está acabado con materiales no tóxicos y está equipado con una chimenea de gas y tragaluces operables. A pesar de su tamaño, el interior de esta casa se siente espacioso, está bañado en luz natural y tiene espacio para un generoso espacio de trabajo, que ha sido tallado en la ventana del espacio habitable principal. La casa ofrece mucho espacio de almacenamiento y muebles polivalentes y móviles para maximizar la funcionalidad y la habitabilidad.

STUDIO BEN ALLEN

BEN ALLEN, TOP NOTCH JOINERY,
FORMAT ENGINEERS, DANIEL BELL LANDSKAP,
SULLIVAN AND COMPANY, HUB WORKSHOP

www.studiobenallen.com

Founded by architect Ben Allen in 2014 after 15+ years of experience collaborating with designers, architects, artists and other creative disciplines, Studio Ben Allen is a multidisciplinary design practice known for its unique and engaging spaces. At the core of Studio Ben Allen's creative design lies an open and collaborative dialogue between the participant and the disciplines. Listed as one of the top 20 emerging architects globally by Dezeen in 2018, Studio Ben Allen has won a number of design awards in the past few years.

Das Studio Ben Allen wurde 2014 von dem Architekten Ben Allen gegründet, nachdem er mehr als 15 Jahre Erfahrung in der Zusammenarbeit mit Designern, Architekten, Künstlern und anderen kreativen Disziplinen gesammelt hatte. Das Studio Ben Allen ist ein multidisziplinäres Designbüro, das für seine einzigartigen und ansprechenden Räume bekannt ist. Im Mittelpunkt des kreativen Designs von Studio Ben Allen steht ein offener und gemeinschaftlicher Dialog zwischen den Teilnehmern und den Disziplinen. Das Studio Ben Allen wurde 2018 von Dezeen als einer der 20 besten aufstrebenden Architekten weltweit gelistet und hat in den letzten Jahren mehrere Designpreise gewonnen.

A ROOM FOR ONE MORE

A ROOM IN THE GARDEN

Fondé par l'architecte Ben Allen en 2014 après plus de 15 ans d'expérience de collaboration avec des designers, des architectes, des artistes et d'autres disciplines créatives, le Studio Ben Allen est un bureau de design multidisciplinaire connu pour ses espaces uniques et engageants. Au cœur de la conception créative du Studio Ben Allen se trouve un dialogue ouvert et collaboratif entre le participant et les disciplines. Classé parmi les 20 meilleurs architectes émergents au niveau mondial par Dezeen en 2018, le Studio Ben Allen a remporté plusieurs prix de design ces dernières années.

Fundado por el arquitecto Ben Allen en 2014 tras más de 15 años de experiencia colaborando con diseñadores, arquitectos, artistas y otras disciplinas creativas, Studio Ben Allen es una oficina de diseño multidisciplinar conocido por sus espacios únicos y atractivos. En el núcleo del diseño creativo de Studio Ben Allen se encuentra un diálogo abierto y colaborativo entre el participante y las disciplinas. Catalogado como uno de los 20 mejores arquitectos emergentes a nivel global por Dezeen en 2018, Studio Ben Allen ha ganado varios premios de diseño en los últimos años.

A ROOM FOR ONE MORE

LONDON, UNITED KINGDOM

PHOTOS © FRENCH & TYE

The owner of this flat in central London's Barbican Estate reached out to Studio Ben Allen to find space for a children's bedroom, a workspace and additional storage within the existing layout. They also requested a flexible intervention that would reflect the architecture of the Barbican and allow the modest-sized flat to accommodate the growing family. To create a second bedroom, an architectural element is inserted in the middle of the apartment to create a wall and a door. The structure serves as a workspace with a drop-down desk and home office storage on one side and a bed, child's desk and seating area on the other side. The design allows for the space to be used and arranged in multiple ways. The desk, supported by a cable and operated with a counterweight, can be folded away when not in use, while the cupboards above and below the desk serve as storage for the home or work.

Der Eigentümer dieser Wohnung in Londons zentralem Barbican-Viertel wandte sich an das Studio Ben Allen, um Platz für ein Kinderzimmer, einen Arbeitsbereich und zusätzlichen Stauraum in den vorhandenen Räumlichkeiten zu finden. Außerdem wünschten sie sich einen flexiblen Eingriff, der die Architektur des Barbican widerspiegelt und es der bescheidenen Wohnung ermöglicht, die wachsende Familie unterzubringen. Um ein zweites Schlafzimmer zu schaffen, wird ein architektonisches Element in die Mitte der Wohnung eingefügt, um eine Wand und einen Durchgang zu schaffen. Die Struktur dient als Arbeitsbereich, mit einem ausklappbaren Schreibtisch und Stauraum auf der einen Seite und einem Bett, einem Kinderschreibtisch und einer Sitzecke auf der anderen Seite. Das Design erlaubt es, den Raum auf vielfältige Weise zu nutzen und zu organisieren. Der durch ein Kabel gestützte und durch ein Gegengewicht angetriebene Schreibtisch kann bei Nichtgebrauch zusammengeklappt werden, während die Schränke über und unter dem Schreibtisch als Stauraum für den Wohn- oder Arbeitsbereich dienen.

Le propriétaire de cet appartement situé dans le quartier central de Barbican à Londres a contacté le Studio Ben Allen pour trouver de l'espace pour une chambre d'enfant, un espace de travail et des rangements supplémentaires dans la disposition existante. Ils ont également demandé une intervention flexible qui refléterait l'architecture de la Barbacane et permettrait à l'appartement de taille modeste d'accueillir la famille grandissante. Pour créer une deuxième chambre, un élément architectural est inséré au centre de l'appartement pour créer un mur et une porte. La structure sert d'espace de travail, avec un bureau pliable et un espace de rangement de bureau d'un côté, et un lit, un bureau pour enfants et un coin salon de l'autre côté. La conception permet d'utiliser et d'organiser l'espace de multiples façons. Le bureau, soutenu par un câble et alimenté par un contrepoids, peut être replié lorsqu'il n'est pas utilisé, tandis que les armoires situées au-dessus et au-dessous du bureau servent de rangement pour la maison ou l'espace de travail.

El propietario de este piso en el céntrico barrio londinense de Barbican se puso en contacto con Studio Ben Allen para encontrar espacio para un dormitorio infantil, un espacio de trabajo y almacenamiento adicional dentro de la distribución existente. También solicitaron una intervención flexible que reflejara la arquitectura del Barbican y permitiera que el piso, de tamaño modesto, acogiera a la creciente familia. Para crear un segundo dormitorio, se inserta un elemento arquitectónico en el centro del apartamento para crear una pared y una puerta. La estructura sirve como espacio de trabajo, con un escritorio desplegable y un espacio de almacenamiento para la oficina en un lado, y una cama, un escritorio para niños y una zona de asientos en el otro. El diseño permite utilizar y organizar el espacio de múltiples maneras. El escritorio, sostenido por un cable y accionado con un contrapeso, se puede plegar cuando no se utiliza, mientras que los armarios situados encima y debajo del escritorio sirven de almacenamiento para el hogar o para el espacio de trabajo.

BALDESSARI
Chris Burden

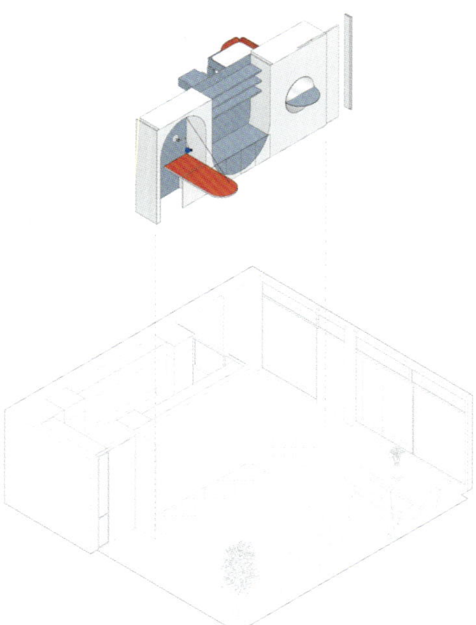

Exploded diagram

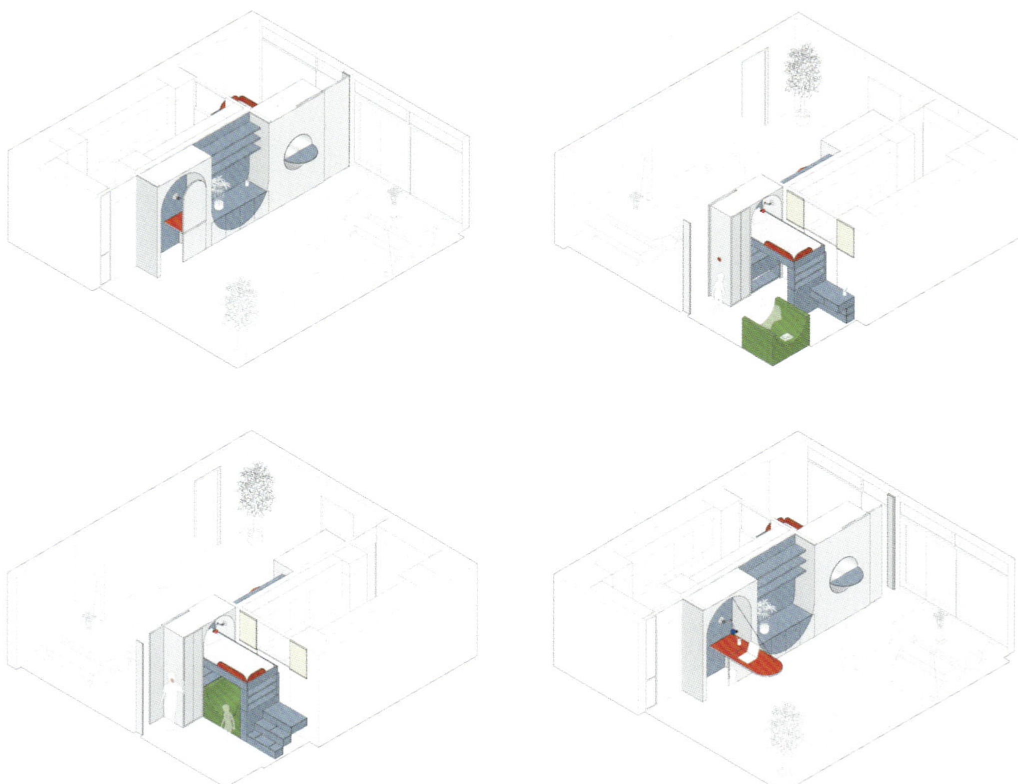

Diagrams

A ROOM IN THE GARDEN

LONDON, UNITED KINGDOM

PHOTOS © BEN TYNEGATE

A Room in the Garden was designed for a family with two young children living in a small garden flat in Putney, in southwest London. Outgrowing their current flat, the family is resisting the urge to move to the suburbs. This piece of architecture is a temporary solution to an overcrowded home, and provide a space for family members to work, play, read, sleep or enjoy a bit of peace and quiet. Less than 15 m^2 in surface area, this sustainable structure is simple enough for self-build assembly and can be fully demounted and re-erected. It comes as a flat pack kit of parts, is fully fabricated on a CNC machine and is made with ultra-low VOC materials. The playful building with its interplay of changing geometric forms and green cladding can partially blend in to its natural surroundings. Inside the octagonal wall structure rises to form a hexagonal roof which frames a square skylight. A large window on one side offers views and lets in more light.

Das Projekt wurde für eine Familie mit zwei kleinen Kindern entworfen, die in einer kleinen Gartenwohnung in Putney im Südwesten Londons lebt. Die Familie zögert, in einen Vorort zu ziehen, obwohl ihre jetzige Wohnung zu klein für sie ist. Dieses architektonische Werk ist eine vorübergehende Lösung für eine überfüllte Wohnung und bietet den Familienmitgliedern einen Raum zum Arbeiten, Spielen, Lesen, Schlafen oder um Ruhe und Frieden zu genießen. Mit einer Grundfläche von weniger als 15 m^2 ist diese nachhaltige Struktur einfach genug, um sie selbst zu montieren, und sie kann vollständig demontiert und wieder aufgebaut werden. Er wird als Bausatz mit flachen Teilen geliefert, vollständig auf einer CNC-Maschine hergestellt und besteht aus Materialien mit sehr geringen VOC-Emissionen. Das verspielte Gebäude mit seinem Spiel aus wechselnden geometrischen Formen und grüner Verkleidung kann teilweise in die natürliche Umgebung integriert werden. Im Inneren steigt die achteckige Wandstruktur zu einem sechseckigen Dach an, das ein quadratisches Oberlicht einrahmt. Ein großes Fenster auf einer Seite bietet Aussicht und lässt mehr Licht herein.

Le projet a été conçu pour une famille avec deux jeunes enfants vivant dans un petit appartement avec jardin à Putney, dans le sud-ouest de Londres. La famille hésite à déménager en banlieue, même si son appartement actuel est trop petit pour elle. Cette pièce d'architecture est une solution temporaire à une maison surpeuplée et offre un espace aux membres de la famille pour travailler, jouer, lire, dormir ou profiter d'un peu de paix et de tranquillité. Avec moins de 15 m^2 de surface au sol, cette structure durable est assez simple à monter soi-même et peut être entièrement démontée et remontée. Il se présente sous la forme d'un kit de pièces à plat, est entièrement fabriqué sur une machine à commande numérique et est composé de matériaux à très faible émission de COV. Le bâtiment ludique, avec son jeu de formes géométriques changeantes et son revêtement vert, peut être partiellement intégré dans son environnement naturel. À l'intérieur, la structure octogonale des murs s'élève pour former un toit hexagonal encadrant un puits de lumière carré. Une grande fenêtre sur un côté offre des vues et laisse entrer plus de lumière.

El proyecto fue diseñado para una familia con dos niños pequeños que viven en un pequeño piso con jardín en Putney, en el suroeste de Londres. La familia se resiste a mudarse a las afueras, aunque su piso actual se les queda pequeño. Esta pieza arquitectónica es una solución temporal a un hogar superpoblado, y proporciona un espacio para que los miembros de la familia trabajen, jueguen, lean, duerman o disfruten de un poco de paz y tranquilidad. Con menos de 15 m^2 de superficie, esta estructura sostenible es lo suficientemente sencilla como para ser montada por uno mismo y puede desmontarse y volverse a montar por completo. Se presenta como un kit de piezas en paquete plano, se fabrica completamente en una máquina CNC y se hace con materiales de muy baja emisión de COV. El edificio, de carácter lúdico, con su juego de formas geométricas cambiantes y su revestimiento verde, puede integrarse parcialmente en su entorno natural. En el interior, la estructura de la pared octogonal se eleva para formar un techo hexagonal que enmarca un tragaluz cuadrado. Un gran ventanal en uno de los lados ofrece vistas y deja entrar más luz.

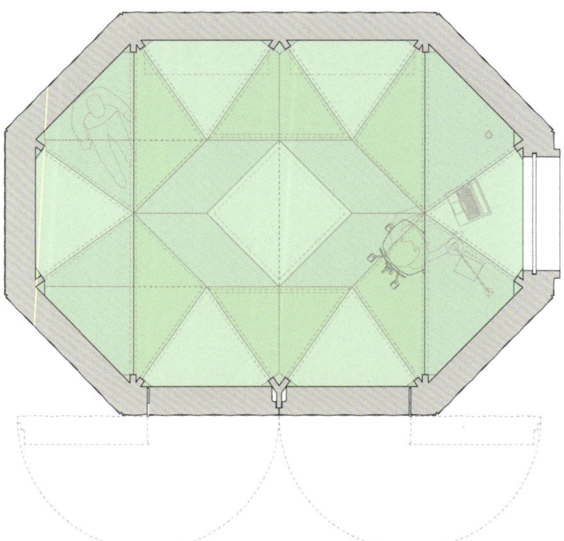

Front elevation

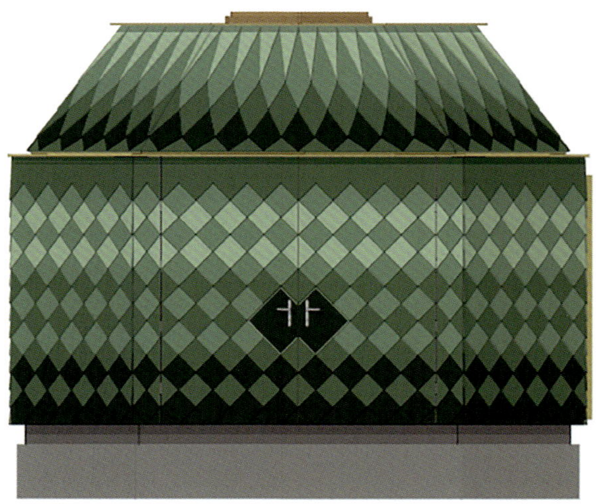

Front elevation

SUSANNA COTS INTERIOR DESIGN

© Elena Alonso

SUSANNA COTS

www.susannacots.com

For Susanna Cots, living in a medieval village in Catalonia's natural Empordà region strengthens the way she understands spaces and the way she works with light and smells. For over 20 years she has created balanced, comfortable and timeless interiors, free from clichés and frills, and full of concept and emotion. "Light is the main invisible element that can guide our emotions," says Susanna, and it plays a key role in her designs. She has a unique way of incorporating light, feelings and nature into conscious, pleasant and mindful interiors. For this Catalan designer, a good interior needs to have a layout that is easy to move around in and without any sharp angles. It should be a place that invites you to stay and evoke a mood, through smells or light. For Susanna Cots, working with natural materials is like working with the pure essence and being conscious of not contaminating. Her essence is minimal expression with maximum emotion.

Susanna Cots lebt in einem mittelalterlichen Dorf in der natürlichen Region Empordà in Katalonien, was ihr Verständnis von Räumen und die Arbeit mit Licht und Gerüchen stärkt. Seit mehr als 20 Jahren kreiert sie ausgewogene, komfortable und zeitlose Innenräume, ohne Klischees und Schnickschnack, voller Konzept und Emotionen. „Licht ist das wichtigste unsichtbare Element, das unsere Emotionen steuern kann", sagt Susanna, und es spielt in ihren Entwürfen eine grundlegende Rolle. Sie hat eine einzigartige Art, Licht, Gefühle und Natur in bewusste, angenehme und bewusste Innenräume zu integrieren. Für den katalanischen Designer sollte eine gute Inneneinrichtung ein leicht zu bewegendes Layout ohne scharfe Winkel haben. Es sollte ein Ort sein, der zum Verweilen einlädt und einen Gemütszustand hervorruft, durch Gerüche oder Licht. Für Susanna Cots ist die Arbeit mit natürlichen Materialien gleichbedeutend mit der Arbeit mit der reinen Essenz und dem Bewusstsein, nichts zu verschmutzen. Ihre Essenz ist ein Minimum an Ausdruck mit einem Maximum an Emotion.

COPPER HOUSE

DAWN HOUSE

Pour Susanna Cots, vivre dans un village médiéval de la région naturelle de l'Empordà, en Catalogne, renforce sa façon de comprendre les espaces et de travailler avec la lumière et les odeurs. Depuis plus de 20 ans, elle crée des intérieurs équilibrés, confortables et intemporels, sans clichés ni fioritures, et pleins de concepts et d'émotions. « La lumière est le principal élément invisible qui peut guider nos émotions », explique Susanna, et elle joue un rôle fondamental dans ses créations. Elle a une façon unique d'incorporer la lumière, les sentiments et la nature dans des intérieurs conscients, agréables et conscients. Pour ce designer catalan, un bon intérieur doit avoir une disposition facile à déplacer, sans angles aigus. Ce doit être un lieu qui vous invite à vous attarder et qui évoque un état d'esprit, par les odeurs ou la lumière. Pour Susanna Cots, travailler avec des matériaux naturels, c'est comme travailler avec une essence pure et être conscient de ne pas polluer. Son essence est l'expression minimale avec l'émotion maximale.

Para Susanna Cots, vivir en un pueblo medieval del Empordà natural de Cataluña refuerza su forma de entender los espacios y de trabajar con la luz y los olores. Desde hace más de 20 años crea interiores equilibrados, confortables y atemporales, sin tópicos ni florituras, y llenos de concepto y emoción. «La luz es el principal elemento invisible que puede guiar nuestras emociones», dice Susanna, y desempeña un papel fundamental en sus diseños. Tiene una forma única de incorporar la luz, los sentimientos y la naturaleza en interiores conscientes, agradables y conscientes. Para esta diseñadora catalana, un buen interior debe tener una distribución fácil de mover y sin ángulos agudos. Debe ser un lugar que invite a quedarse y que evoque un estado de ánimo, a través de los olores o la luz. Para Susanna Cots, trabajar con materiales naturales es como trabajar con la esencia pura y ser consciente de no contaminar. Su esencia es la mínima expresión con la máxima emoción.

COPPER HOUSE

EMPORDÀ, COSTA BRAVA, SPAIN

PHOTOS © MAURICIO FUERTES

This minimalist family home honours the earthy colour, texture and security of copper. It is a visually pleasing and calm interior that evokes emotional wellbeing. As well as copper, light and the colour white dominate in this interior design. Connecting the interior with the exterior not only floods this home with daylight, it also allows the interior and its occupants to interact with every season of the year. White offers silence to the mix of earthy colours and textures used throughout. The ground floor office space lined with oak is connected to the open-plan living-dining-kitchen area by a copper-framed glass partition continuing the interior-exterior connection. The bespoke desk with copper legs reminiscent of jewellery design matches the breakfast bar in the kitchen and adds a light and airy touch to a space dominated by the earthy texture and colour of oak.

Cette maison familiale minimaliste rend hommage à la couleur terreuse, à la texture et à la sécurité du cuivre. C'est un intérieur visuellement agréable et tranquille qui évoque le bien-être émotionnel. En plus du cuivre, la lumière et le blanc dominent cette décoration intérieure. La connexion de l'intérieur avec l'extérieur n'inonde pas seulement cette maison de lumière naturelle, mais permet également à l'intérieur et à ses occupants d'interagir avec chaque saison de l'année. Le blanc offre un silence au mélange de couleurs et de textures terreuses utilisé dans tout le bâtiment. L'espace de bureaux du rez-de-chaussée, revêtu de chêne, est relié à l'espace ouvert salon-salle à manger-cuisine par une cloison vitrée à ossature en cuivre qui poursuit le lien entre l'intérieur et l'extérieur. Le bureau sur mesure, dont les pieds en cuivre rappellent le design des bijoux, est assorti au bar de la cuisine et ajoute une touche de lumière et d'air à un espace dominé par la texture et la couleur terreuses du chêne.

Dieses minimalistische Familienhaus ist eine Hommage an die erdige Farbe, Textur und Sicherheit von Kupfer. Es ist ein visuell ansprechendes und ruhiges Interieur, das emotionales Wohlbefinden hervorruft. Neben Kupfer dominieren Licht und Weiß diese Inneneinrichtung. Die Verbindung des Innenraums mit dem Außenbereich durchflutet dieses Haus nicht nur mit natürlichem Licht, sondern ermöglicht es dem Innenraum und seinen Bewohnern auch, mit jeder Jahreszeit zu interagieren. Weiß bietet einen Ausgleich zu der Mischung aus erdigen Farben und Texturen, die im gesamten Gebäude verwendet werden. Der mit Eichenholz verkleidete Büroraum im Erdgeschoss ist durch eine kupfergerahmte Glastrennwand mit dem offenen Wohn-Ess-Küchenbereich verbunden, die die Verbindung zwischen Innen- und Außenbereich fortführt. Der maßgefertigte Schreibtisch mit kupfernen Beinen, die an Schmuckdesign erinnern, passt zur Frühstückstheke in der Küche und bringt einen Hauch von Licht und Luft in einen Raum, der von der erdigen Textur und Farbe der Eiche dominiert wird.

Esta casa familiar minimalista hace honor al color terroso, la textura y la seguridad del cobre. Es un interior visualmente agradable y tranquilo que evoca el bienestar emocional. Además del cobre, la luz y el color blanco dominan en este diseño interior. La conexión del interior con el exterior no sólo inunda esta casa de luz natural, sino que también permite que el interior y sus ocupantes interactúen con cada estación del año. El blanco ofrece silencio a la mezcla de colores terrosos y texturas utilizadas en todo el edificio. El espacio de oficina de la planta baja, revestido de roble, está conectado con el salón-comedor-cocina de planta abierta mediante un tabique de cristal con marco de cobre que continúa la conexión entre el interior y el exterior. El escritorio hecho a medida con patas de cobre que recuerdan al diseño de joyas hace juego con la barra de desayuno de la cocina y añade un toque de luz y aire a un espacio dominado por la textura y el color terrosos del roble.

DAWN HOUSE

MANRESA, SPAIN

PHOTOS © MAURICIO FUERTES

Located at the foot of the imposing Montserrat mountains, the magic and light of the natural surroundings served as an inspiration for the interior design of this family home. Further inspiration is drawn from the colour white, the need for a space with well-being and comfort at the core, and a home that allows the family to be connected in spite of separate personal spaces. Each floor in this house has a different intention. Thus, the open ground floor is the main living area with the kitchen connecting to the dining and living room. The entire first floor is dedicated to the young teenagers of this family, with individual spaces reflecting each personality. The suite takes up the whole top floor. It features an open, yet intimate space with a bathroom and dressing room on one end of the space. A glass fish tank on the opposite end of the room allows creates space for a small home office, with incredible sunrise views.

Située au pied des imposantes montagnes de Montserrat, la magie et la lumière de l'environnement naturel ont inspiré le design intérieur de cette maison familiale. La couleur blanche, le besoin d'un espace dans lequel le bien-être et le confort sont l'axe central, et une maison qui permet à la famille d'être connectée malgré des espaces personnels séparés, sont d'autres sources d'inspiration. Chaque étage de cette maison a une intention différente. Ainsi, le rez-de-chaussée ouvert constitue la principale pièce à vivre, la cuisine étant reliée à la salle à manger et au salon. Le premier étage est entièrement consacré aux jeunes adolescents de cette famille, avec des espaces individuels reflétant chaque personnalité. La suite occupe tout le dernier étage. L'espace est ouvert mais intime, avec une salle de bain et un dressing à une extrémité de l'espace. Un aquarium en verre à l'autre bout de la pièce crée un petit espace de bureau avec une vue imprenable sur le lever du soleil.

Am Fuße des imposanten Montserrat-Gebirges gelegen, inspirierten der Zauber und das Licht der natürlichen Umgebung die Inneneinrichtung dieses Familienhauses. Weitere Inspirationsquellen sind die Farbe Weiß, das Bedürfnis nach einem Raum, in dem Wohlbefinden und Komfort im Mittelpunkt stehen, und ein Haus, das es der Familie ermöglicht, trotz getrennter persönlicher Räume miteinander verbunden zu sein. Jedes Stockwerk dieses Hauses hat einen anderen Zweck. So ist das offene Erdgeschoss der Hauptwohnbereich, wobei die Küche mit dem Esszimmer und dem Wohnzimmer verbunden ist. Die gesamte erste Etage ist den jungen Teenagern dieser Familie gewidmet, mit individuellen Räumen, die jede Persönlichkeit widerspiegeln. Die Suite nimmt das gesamte Dachgeschoss ein. Der Raum ist offen und doch intim, mit einem Badezimmer und einem Ankleidezimmer an einem Ende des Raumes. Ein gläsernes Aquarium am gegenüberliegenden Ende des Raumes schafft einen kleinen Büroraum mit herrlichem Blick auf den Sonnenaufgang.

Situada al pie de las imponentes montañas de Montserrat, la magia y la luz del entorno natural sirvieron de inspiración para el diseño interior de esta casa familiar. El color blanco, la necesidad de un espacio en el que el bienestar y el confort sean el eje central, y un hogar que permita a la familia estar conectada a pesar de tener espacios personales separados, son otras de las fuentes de inspiración. Cada planta de esta casa tiene una intención diferente. Así, la planta baja abierta es la zona de estar principal, con la cocina conectada al comedor y al salón. Toda la primera planta está dedicada a los jóvenes adolescentes de esta familia, con espacios individuales que reflejan cada personalidad. La suite ocupa toda la planta superior. Cuenta con un espacio abierto, pero íntimo, con un baño y un vestidor en un extremo del espacio. Una pecera de cristal en el extremo opuesto de la habitación permite crear un espacio para una pequeña oficina con increíbles vistas al amanecer.

MUSES
KINFOLK

TG STUDIO

THOMAS GRIEM

www.tg-studio.co.uk

With over 20 years of design experience, German-born Thomas Griem has worked on numerous residential, retail and office schemes all over the world, from the UK to New York, Hong Kong, Moscow and Ibiza. Thomas Griem worked with Phillippe Stark for the global residential developer YOO at the end of the nineties and, together with Tara Bernard, he co-founded the successful interior design practice Target Living. Based in Hampstead, London, today TG Studio works on a wide range of projects, including penthouses in Central London, an English country estate, a villa in Saint Tropez and a private lodge in Montana.

Der in Deutschland geborene Thomas Griem verfügt über mehr als 20 Jahre Designerfahrung und hat an zahlreichen Wohn-, Einzelhandels- und Büroprojekten auf der ganzen Welt mitgewirkt, von Großbritannien bis New York, Hongkong, Moskau und Ibiza. Ende der neunziger Jahre arbeitete Thomas Griem mit Phillippe Stark für den globalen Wohnentwickler YOO und gründete zusammen mit Tara Bernard das erfolgreiche Innenarchitekturbüro Target Living. Heute arbeitet TG Studio mit Sitz in Hampstead, London, an einer Vielzahl von Projekten, darunter Penthäuser im Zentrum Londons, ein englischer Landsitz, eine Villa in Saint Tropez und eine private Lodge in Montana.

HONG KONG OFFICE

HOLLY LODGE

Avec plus de 20 ans d'expérience en design, Thomas Griem, né en Allemagne, a travaillé sur de nombreux projets résidentiels, commerciaux et de bureaux dans le monde entier, du Royaume-Uni à New York, Hong Kong, Moscou et Ibiza. Thomas Griem a travaillé avec Phillippe Stark pour le promoteur résidentiel mondial YOO à la fin des années 90 et, avec Tara Bernard, il a cofondé le cabinet d'architecture d'intérieur Target Living. Basé à Hampstead, Londres, TG Studio travaille aujourd'hui sur un large éventail de projets, dont des penthouses dans le centre de Londres, une propriété de campagne anglaise, une villa à Saint-Tropez et un pavillon privé dans le Montana.

Con más de 20 años de experiencia en diseño, el alemán Thomas Griem ha trabajado en numerosos proyectos residenciales, comerciales y de oficinas en todo el mundo, desde el Reino Unido hasta Nueva York, Hong Kong, Moscú e Ibiza. Thomas Griem trabajó con Phillippe Stark para el promotor residencial mundial YOO a finales de los noventa y, junto con Tara Bernard, co fundó el exitoso estudio de diseño de interiores Target Living. Con sede en Hampstead (Londres), el estudio TG trabaja hoy en una amplia gama de proyectos, como áticos en el centro de Londres, una finca inglesa, una villa en Saint Tropez y un alojamiento privado en Montana.

HONG KONG OFFICE

HONG KONG, CHINA

PHOTOS © PHILIP VILE

The high-profile client of this inviting and functional home office in the heart of Hong Kong requested an office with a touch of Britishness and 1960s flair. The space is primarily used for work, but with the possibility to host clients in a more intimate setting. Just under 15 m², the room is divided into an office area and an intimate meeting space. One side of the room is dominated by a custom-designed desk made of cherry wood with brass connections ad a leather writing pad recessed into the top. Office equipment, cable management and an air purifier are concealed within the desk. A Vitra Eames chair upholstered in soft cream leather adds a classic touch. Bringing forward the wall line allowed for storage units to run the length of the wall. A curved sofa designed by TG Studio fits perfectly in the alcove and takes prime position in the lounge area complemented by the brutalist 1970s coffee table by furniture sculptor Silas Seandel.

Le client très en vue de ce bureau à domicile accueillant et fonctionnel situé au cœur de Hong Kong souhaitait un bureau avec une touche britannique et un style des années 1960. L'espace est principalement utilisé pour le travail, mais avec la possibilité d'accueillir des clients dans un cadre plus intime. D'une superficie d'un peu moins de 15 m², la pièce est divisée en une zone de bureaux et un espace de réunion intime. L'un des côtés de la pièce est dominé par un bureau conçu sur mesure en bois de cerisier avec des connexions en laiton et un bloc-notes en cuir encastré dans le dessus. L'équipement de bureau, la gestion des câbles et un purificateur d'air sont dissimulés dans le bureau. Une chaise Vitra Eames recouverte d'un cuir crème souple ajoute une touche classique. Le fait d'avancer la ligne du mur a permis d'installer des unités de rangement sur toute la longueur du mur. Un canapé incurvé conçu par TG Studio s'adapte parfaitement à l'alcôve et occupe une place de choix dans le salon, complété par la table basse brutaliste des années 1970 du sculpteur de meubles Silas Seandel.

Der hochkarätige Kunde dieses einladenden und funktionalen Heimbüros im Herzen Hongkongs wünschte sich ein Büro mit einem Hauch von Britishness und dem Flair der 1960er Jahre. Der Raum wird hauptsächlich zum Arbeiten genutzt, bietet aber auch die Möglichkeit, Kunden in einem intimeren Rahmen zu empfangen. Der knapp 15 m² große Raum ist in einen Bürobereich und einen intimen Besprechungsbereich unterteilt. Eine Seite des Raums wird von einem maßgefertigten Schreibtisch aus Kirschholz mit Messinganschlüssen und einer in die Platte eingelassenen Lederschreibunterlage dominiert. Bürogeräte, Kabelmanagement und ein Luftreiniger sind in dem Schreibtisch verborgen. Ein mit weichem, cremefarbenem Leder bezogener Eames Chair von Vitra verleiht dem Raum eine klassische Note. Durch das Vorziehen der Wandlinie konnten Stauraummöbel über die gesamte Länge der Wand verteilt werden. Ein geschwungenes Sofa, das von TG Studio entworfen wurde, passt perfekt in die Nische und nimmt den ersten Platz in der Lounge ein, ergänzt durch den brutalistischen 1970er-Jahre-Couchtisch des Möbelbauers Silas Seandel.

El cliente de alto perfil de esta acogedora y funcional oficina en casa en el corazón de Hong Kong pidió un espacio de trabajo con un toque británico de los años 60. El espacio se utiliza principalmente para trabajar, pero con la posibilidad de recibir a clientes en un entorno más íntimo. Con algo menos de 15 m², la sala se divide en una zona de oficina y un espacio de reunión íntimo. Uno de los lados de la sala está dominado por un escritorio diseñado a medida, hecho de madera de cerezo con conexiones de latón y un bloc de notas de cuero empotrado en la parte superior. El equipo de oficina, la gestión de los cables y un purificador de aire están ocultos dentro del escritorio. Una silla Eames de Vitra tapizada en suave piel color crema añade un toque clásico. El adelanto de la línea de la pared ha permitido que los armarios se extiendan a lo largo de la misma. Un sofá curvado diseñado por TG Studio encaja perfectamente en la alcoba, ocupando una posición privilegiada en la zona del salón, complementada a su vez por la mesa de centro de estilo brutalista de los años 70 del escultor de muebles Silas Seandel.

BEST
THE IMPOSSIBLE
COLLECTION OF

ESCAPE
HOTEL STORIES
7

HOLLY LODGE

LONDON, UNITED KINGDOM

PHOTOS © PHILIP VILE

For this grandiose renovation, TG-Studio was asked to join two apartments in a South Kensington mansion block, thus doubling the owner's living space. TG-Studio's proposal was to split the two floors into entertaining floor and an accommodation floor connected to the upstairs through a private staircase. The open-plan entertaining area is accessed via a double-height entrance hall. The study is connected to this living area by a set of mirrored sliding doors. Dominated by a leather-topped antique desk, the elegant office features a mix of vintage and contemporary pieces. Two vintage mirrored wall sconces contrast with a modern photography by Henning Boch and the luxurious and timeless Shear desk lamp by Bert Frank.

Für diese grandiose Renovierung wurde TG-Studio gebeten, zwei Wohnungen in einem Herrenhaus in South Kensington zu verbinden und so die Wohnfläche des Eigentümers zu verdoppeln. TG-Studio schlug vor, die beiden Etagen in eine Unterhaltungsetage und eine Wohnetage aufzuteilen, die über eine private Treppe mit dem Obergeschoss verbunden ist. Der offen gestaltete Wohnbereich wird über eine doppelhohe Eingangshalle erschlossen. Das Arbeitszimmer ist durch verspiegelte Schiebetüren mit diesem Wohnbereich verbunden. Das elegante Büro wird von einem antiken Schreibtisch mit Lederauflage dominiert und ist mit einer Mischung aus Vintage- und zeitgenössischen Möbeln ausgestattet. Zwei verspiegelte Wandleuchten im Vintage-Stil kontrastieren mit einer modernen Fotografie von Henning Boch und der luxuriösen und zeitlosen Schreibtischlampe Shear von Bert Frank.

Pour cette rénovation grandiose, TG-Studio a été chargé de réunir deux appartements dans un hôtel particulier de South Kensington, doublant ainsi l'espace de vie du propriétaire. La proposition de TG-Studio était de diviser les deux étages en un étage de divertissement et un étage d'habitation relié à l'étage supérieur par un escalier privé. L'accès à l'espace de divertissement ouvert se fait par un hall d'entrée à double hauteur. Le bureau est relié à cet espace de vie par un ensemble de portes coulissantes en miroir. Dominé par un bureau ancien à dessus en cuir, l'élégant bureau présente un mélange de pièces vintage et contemporaines. Deux appliques murales vintage en miroir contrastent avec une photographie moderne de Henning Boch et la luxueuse et intemporelle lampe de bureau Shear de Bert Frank.

Para esta grandiosa renovación, se pidió a TG-Studio que uniera dos apartamentos en una mansión de South Kensington, duplicando así el espacio vital del propietario. La propuesta de TG-Studio consistió en dividir los dos pisos en una planta de entretenimiento y una planta de alojamiento conectada a la planta superior a través de una escalera privada. A la zona de ocio de planta abierta se accede a través de un vestíbulo de doble altura. El estudio está conectado a esta zona de estar por un juego de puertas correderas con espejos. Dominado por un escritorio antiguo con tapa de cuero, el elegante despacho presenta una mezcla de piezas vintage y contemporáneas. Dos apliques de pared con espejos antiguos contrastan con una fotografía moderna de Henning Boch y la lujosa e intemporal lámpara de escritorio Shear de Bert Frank.

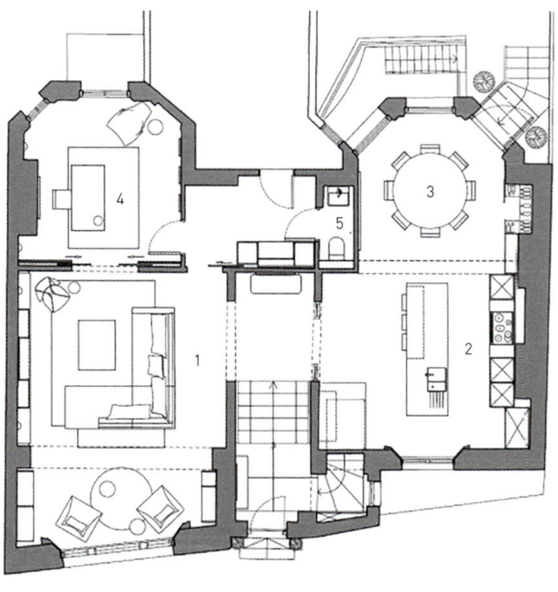

1. Living room
2. Kitchen
3. Dining room
4. Office
5. Guest WC

Floor plan

URBANOLOGY DESIGNS

GINGER CURTIS

www.urbanologydesigns.com

A personal battle with cancer inspired Ginger Curtis to change her home environment to improve her wellness and healing process. Working on the renovation of her own home not only helped her regain energy and a zest for life, it confirmed her love for interior design and opened many new doors for her. In 2015, Ginger Curtis founded Urbanology Designs to inspire and help people have beautiful, comfortable and functional homes. For Ginger Curtis, customer relationship management is key to a successful project. Urbanology Designs gain the clients' trust by communicating everything and managing their expectations. Ginger Curtis pays special attention to the emotional side of a relationship and likes to connect with clients, discovering and understanding the person every step of the way.

Ein persönlicher Kampf gegen den Krebs inspirierte Ginger Curtis dazu, ihr häusliches Umfeld zu verändern, um ihr Wohlbefinden und ihren Heilungsprozess zu verbessern. Die Arbeit an der Renovierung ihres eigenen Hauses hat ihr nicht nur geholfen, ihre Energie und Lebensfreude zurückzugewinnen, sondern auch ihre Liebe zur Innenarchitektur bestätigt und ihr viele neue Türen geöffnet. Im Jahr 2015 gründete Ginger Curtis Urbanology Designs, um Menschen zu inspirieren und ihnen zu helfen, ein schönes, komfortables und funktionales Zuhause zu haben. Für Ginger Curtis ist das Kundenbeziehungsmanagement der Schlüssel zum Erfolg eines Projekts. Urbanology Designs verdient sich das Vertrauen seiner Kunden, indem es alles kommuniziert und ihre Erwartungen erfüllt. Ginger achtet besonders auf die emotionale Seite einer Beziehung und liebt es, mit ihren Kunden in Kontakt zu treten und die Person bei jedem Schritt zu entdecken und zu verstehen.

ASHLEY ROBERTSON

PRESTON HOLLOW

HOCKADAY NEIGHBOURHOOD

Un combat personnel contre le cancer a incité Ginger Curtis à modifier son environnement domestique pour améliorer son bien-être et son processus de guérison. Travailler à la rénovation de sa propre maison l'a non seulement aidée à retrouver son énergie et sa joie de vivre, mais a confirmé son amour de la décoration intérieure et lui a ouvert de nombreuses portes. En 2015, Ginger Curtis a fondé Urbanology Designs pour inspirer et aider les gens à avoir des maisons belles, confortables et fonctionnelles. Pour Ginger Curtis, la gestion des relations avec les clients est essentielle à la réussite d'un projet. Urbanology Designs gagne la confiance de ses clients en communiquant tout et en gérant leurs attentes. Ginger accorde une attention particulière à l'aspect émotionnel d'une relation et aime établir un lien avec les clients, en découvrant et en comprenant la personne à chaque étape du processus.

Una batalla personal contra el cáncer inspiró a Ginger Curtis a cambiar su entorno doméstico para mejorar su bienestar y su proceso de curación. Trabajar en la renovación de su propia casa no solo la ayudó a recuperar la energía y las ganas de vivir, sino que confirmó su amor por el diseño de interiores y le abrió muchas puertas nuevas. En 2015, Ginger Curtis fundó Urbanology Designs para inspirar y ayudar a las personas a tener hogares hermosos, cómodos y funcionales. Para Ginger Curtis, la gestión de la relación con el cliente es clave para el éxito de un proyecto. Urbanology Designs se gana la confianza de los clientes comunicando todo y gestionando sus expectativas. Ginger presta especial atención a la parte emocional de una relación y le gusta conectar con los clientes, descubriendo y entendiendo a la persona en cada paso del camino.

ASHLEY ROBERTSON

DALLAS, TEXAS, UNITED STATES

PHOTOS © MARY HAFNER

This uber chic residence in Dallas, Texas, was designed for influencer and blogger Ashley Robertson and her husband and two sons. The brief was to create a liveable and comfortable family home and the perfect place from which to tell stories and communicate her brand and business. The home office needed to fit this brief more than anything. Ahsley Robertson's work space needed to be both photo-worthy and functional. The bookcase in this uber chic, modern glamorous office is a compelling backdrop for photos, video and content creation. It is lined with dark grass cloth wallpaper and contrasted with white shelves and art work that pops out. The dramatic backdrop is further contrasted by a natural and organic desk and Kisabeth chairs, adding a quality of calm and productivity.

Dieses superstylische Haus in Dallas, Texas, wurde für die Influencerin und Bloggerin Ashley Robertson, ihren Mann und ihre zwei Kinder entworfen. Ziel war es, ein wohnliches und komfortables Haus für die Familie zu schaffen und den perfekten Ort, um Geschichten zu erzählen und ihre Marke und ihr Unternehmen zu kommunizieren. Das Homeoffice musste vor allem diese Anforderung erfüllen. Der Arbeitsbereich von Ahsley Robertson musste fotogen und funktional sein. Die Regale in diesem glamourösen, modernen und sehr stilvollen Büro bilden eine attraktive Kulisse für Fotos, Videos und die Erstellung von Inhalten. Er ist mit dunkler Grastuch-Tapete ausgekleidet und wird durch weiße Regale und hervorstehende Kunstwerke kontrastiert. Die dramatische Kulisse wird durch einen natürlichen, organischen Schreibtisch und Kisabeth-Stühle kontrastiert, die für Ruhe und Produktivität sorgen.

Cette résidence super stylée de Dallas, au Texas, a été conçue pour l'influenceuse et blogueuse Ashley Robertson, son mari et ses deux enfants. L'objectif était de créer une maison familiale agréable à vivre et confortable, ainsi que l'endroit idéal pour raconter des histoires et communiquer sur leur marque et leur activité. Le bureau à domicile devait avant tout répondre à cette exigence. L'espace de travail d'Ahsley Robertson devait être digne d'être photographié et fonctionnel. Les étagères de ce bureau glamour, moderne et très élégant constituent une toile de fond attrayante pour les photos, les vidéos et la création de contenu. Elle est tapissée d'un papier peint sombre en toile de gazon et contrastée par des étagères blanches et des œuvres d'art en saillie. La toile de fond dramatique est encore contrastée par un bureau naturel et organique et des chaises Kisabeth, qui apportent calme et productivité.

Esta residencia súper elegante en Dallas, Texas, fue diseñada para la influencer y bloguera Ashley Robertson y su marido y dos hijos. El objetivo era crear una casa familiar habitable y confortable y el lugar perfecto para contar historias y comunicar su marca y su negocio. La oficina en casa tenía que ajustarse a este requisito por encima de todo. El espacio de trabajo de Ahsley Robertson tenía que ser digno de ser fotografiado y funcional. La estantería de esta oficina glamurosa, moderna y muy elegante, es un atractivo telón de fondo para las fotos, los vídeos y la creación de contenidos. Está revestida con papel pintado de tela de hierba oscura y contrastada con estantes blancos y obras de arte que sobresalen. El dramático telón de fondo se contrasta además con un escritorio natural y orgánico y las sillas Kisabeth, que añaden calma y productividad.

PRESTON HOLLOW

DALLAS, TEXAS, UNITED STATES

PHOTOS © MATTI GRESHAM

The owners of this 5,000-square-foot home in Dallas, Texas, wanted a functional and pet-friendly home for them to enjoy and entertain from. The result is a relaxed, modern style with a subtle use of colours and artwork throughout. The office was designed for the husband's use and incorporates his love of luxury cars. An existing built-in on the back wall displays a selection of vintage cars alongside books, sculptural items and artwork. The soft, curved lines of the wooden desk are complemented by a big comfy desk chair covered in an oatmeal velvet fabric. A bench placed against the window provides an area for reading or relaxing and adds texture and colour to this room.

Les propriétaires de cette maison de 465 m^2 située à Dallas, au Texas, voulaient une maison fonctionnelle et adaptée aux animaux de compagnie pour en profiter et recevoir. Le résultat est un style moderne et décontracté, avec une utilisation subtile des couleurs et des œuvres d'art. Le bureau a été conçu pour l'usage du mari et intègre son amour des voitures de luxe. Un meuble encastré sur le mur du fond présente une sélection de voitures anciennes ainsi que des livres, des objets sculptés et des œuvres d'art. Les lignes douces et courbes du bureau en bois sont complétées par une grande et confortable chaise de bureau recouverte d'un tissu en velours de couleur avoine. Un banc placé contre la fenêtre offre un espace pour lire ou se détendre et ajoute de la texture et de la couleur à cette pièce.

Die Eigentümer dieses 465 m^2 großen Hauses in Dallas, Texas, wollten ein funktionales, haustierfreundliches Haus, in dem sie sich wohlfühlen und Gäste empfangen können. Das Ergebnis ist ein entspannter, moderner Stil mit dezentem Einsatz von Farben und Kunstwerken. Das Büro wurde für den Ehemann entworfen und trägt seiner Liebe zu Luxusautos Rechnung. Ein Einbauschrank an der Rückwand zeigt eine Auswahl von Oldtimern sowie Bücher, Skulpturen und Kunstwerke. Die glatten, geschwungenen Linien des Holzschreibtisches werden durch einen großen, bequemen Schreibtischstuhl ergänzt, der mit einem hafermehlfarbenen Samtstoff bezogen ist. Eine Bank vor dem Fenster lädt zum Lesen oder Entspannen ein und verleiht dem Raum Struktur und Farbe.

Los propietarios de esta casa de 465 m^2 en Dallas, Texas, querían una casa funcional y que aceptara mascotas para disfrutarla y entretenerla. El resultado es un estilo relajado y moderno con un uso sutil de los colores y las obras de arte. La oficina se diseñó para el uso del marido e incorpora su amor por los coches de lujo. Un mueble empotrado en la pared del fondo muestra una selección de coches antiguos junto con libros, objetos escultóricos y obras de arte. Las líneas suaves y curvas del escritorio de madera se complementan con una gran y cómoda silla de escritorio cubierta con una tela de terciopelo color avena. Un banco colocado contra la ventana ofrece una zona para leer o relajarse y añade textura y color a esta habitación.

HOCKADAY NEIGHBOURHOOD

DALLAS, TEXAS, UNITED STATES

PHOTOS © MATTI GRESHAM

After their last home was destroyed by a tornado in the Dallas area, this family of four was looking for a new beautiful and comfortable dwelling to call home. Urbanology Designs was inspired by the house's curves and took further insp ration from well-curated European vignettes. A large, metal-frame window not only gives this chic home office a contemporary relaxed feel, it also offers views over the home's front garden and floods this space with natural light. An elegant black Nuevo desk takes centre stage and is complemented by a warm and neutral colour palette throughout the space, creating a serene space to work from home.

Nachdem ihr letztes Haus durch einen Tornado in der Gegend von Dallas zerstört worden war, suchte die vierköpfige Familie nach einer schönen und komfortablen neuen Wohnung, die sie ihr Zuhause nennen konnte. Urbanology Designs ließ sich von den Kurven des Hauses inspirieren und auch von den gut erhaltenen europäischen Vignetten. Ein großes Fenster mit Metallrahmen verleiht diesem stilvollen Büro nicht nur ein modernes und entspanntes Ambiente, sondern bietet auch einen Blick auf den Vorgarten des Hauses und lässt den Raum mit natürlichem Licht durchfluten. Der elegante schwarze Nuevo-Schreibtisch steht im Mittelpunkt und wird durch eine warme, neutrale Farbpalette ergänzt, die einen ruhigen Raum für die Arbeit von zu Hause aus schafft.

Après que leur dernière maison ait été détruite par une tornade dans la région de Dallas, cette famille de quatre personnes était à la recherche d'une nouvelle habitation belle et confortable. Urbanology Designs s'est inspiré des courbes de la maison et s'est également inspiré des vignettes européennes bien conservées. Une grande fenêtre à cadre métallique donne non seulement à cet espace de bureau élégant un aspect contemporain et décontracté, mais offre également des vues sur le jardin avant de la maison et inonde l'espace de lumière naturelle. L'élégant bureau noir Nuevo occupe le devant de la scène et est complété par une palette de couleurs neutres et chaudes, créant ainsi un espace serein pour travailler à la maison.

Después de que su última casa fuera destruida por un tornado en la zona de Dallas, esta familia de cuatro miembros buscaba una nueva vivienda bonita y cómoda a la que llamar hogar. Urbanology Designs se inspiró en las curvas de la casa y se inspiró también en las viñetas europeas, muy bien conservadas. Una gran ventana con marco metálico no sólo da a este elegante espacio de oficina un aire contemporáneo y relajado, sino que también ofrece vistas al jardín delantero de la casa e inunda este espacio de luz natural. El elegante escritorio negro Nuevo es el protagonista y se complementa con una paleta de colores cálidos y neutros en todo el espacio, creando un espacio sereno para trabajar desde casa.

YLAB ARQUITECTOS

TOBIAS LAARMANN, YOLANDA YUSTE LÓPEZ

www.ylab.es

Formed by Tobias Laarmann and Yolanda Yuste López, YLAB Arquitectos is a Barcelona-based Spanish-German architecture and interior design firm with international acclaim. YLAB has worked on a wide range of projects in Europe and Africa and is specialised in residential, commercial and corporate design. Seamlessly merging architecture and interior design with custom furniture, lighting and furnishing, YLAB creates timeless residential spaces that are unique and functional with a focus on the individual.

YLAB Arquitectos, gegründet von Tobias Laarmann und Yolanda Yuste López, ist ein international anerkanntes spanisch-deutsches Architektur- und Innenarchitekturbüro mit Sitz in Barcelona. YLAB hat an einer Vielzahl von Projekten in Europa und Afrika gearbeitet und ist auf Wohn-, Geschäfts- und Unternehmensdesign spezialisiert. Durch die nahtlose Verbindung von Architektur und Innenarchitektur mit maßgeschneiderten Möbeln, Beleuchtung und Dekoration schafft YLAB zeitlose Wohnräume, die einzigartig und funktional sind und den Menschen in den Mittelpunkt stellen.

ARGENTONA

Formé par Tobias Laarmann et Yolanda Yuste López, YLAB Arquitectos est un cabinet d'architecture et de design d'intérieur hispano-allemand de renommée internationale, basé à Barcelone. YLAB a travaillé sur un large éventail de projets en Europe et en Afrique et est spécialisée dans le design résidentiel, commercial et d'entreprise. En combinant harmonieusement l'architecture et le design d'intérieur avec du mobilier, de l'éclairage et de la décoration sur mesure, YLAB crée des espaces résidentiels intemporels, uniques et fonctionnels, en mettant l'accent sur l'individu.

Formado por Tobias Laarmann y Yolanda Yuste López, YLAB Arquitectos es un estudio hispano-alemán de arquitectura y diseño de interiores con sede en Barcelona que goza de reconocimiento internacional. YLAB ha trabajado en una amplia gama de proyectos en Europa y África y está especializado en diseño residencial, comercial y corporativo. Combinando a la perfección la arquitectura y el diseño de interiores con el mobiliario, la iluminación y la decoración a medida, YLAB crea espacios residenciales atemporales que son únicos y funcionales con un enfoque en el individuo.

ARGENTONA

BARCELONA, SPAIN

PHOTOS © YLAB ARQUITECTOS BARCELONA

The remodel of this 97 m² apartment in Barcelona's Gràcia district was heavily influenced by the Norwegian owner's love for design and the city of Barcelona. To connect the interior with the outdoor space and let in as much light in as possible, YLAB recovered the historical gallery and freed up the interior by creating a central open L-shaped space connected to the gallery garden and inner courtyard. Classical functions are segregated into different subzones within the central space and are furnished with flexible furniture islands and integrated cabinetry, which conceal a kitchen workspace, a breakfast zone with small kitchen appliances and a wine/bar corner. A living room shelf system on one side of the space contains a desk area with a computer, while the double windows leading to the gallery provide plenty of natural sunlight and ventilation to this home office area. Furnished with Carl Hansen lounge chairs and a small table, this space can be used in many different ways.

La rénovation de cet appartement de 97 m² dans le quartier de Gràcia à Barcelone a été fortement influencée par l'amour du propriétaire norvégien pour le design et la ville de Barcelone. Pour relier l'intérieur à l'espace extérieur et laisser entrer autant de lumière que possible, YLAB a récupéré la galerie d'origine et libéré l'intérieur en créant un espace central ouvert en forme de L relié au jardin de la galerie et à la cour intérieure. Les fonctions classiques sont réparties en différentes sous-zones au sein de l'espace central et meublées avec des îlots de meubles flexibles et des placards intégrés, qui dissimulent un espace de travail pour la cuisine, un coin petit-déjeuner avec des petits appareils et un coin vin/bar. Un système d'étagères sur un côté de l'espace contient un bureau avec un ordinateur, tandis que les doubles fenêtres donnant sur la galerie fournissent beaucoup de lumière naturelle et de ventilation à cet espace de bureau à domicile. Meublé de fauteuils Carl Hansen et d'une petite table, cet espace peut être utilisé de nombreuses façons différentes.

Die Renovierung dieser 97 m² großen Wohnung in Barcelonas Stadtteil Gràcia wurde stark von der Liebe des norwegischen Eigentümers zum Design und zur Stadt Barcelona beeinflusst. Um den Innenraum mit dem Außenbereich zu verbinden und so viel Licht wie möglich einzulassen, hat YLAB die ursprüngliche Galerie wiederhergestellt und den Innenraum durch die Schaffung eines zentralen, offenen L-förmigen Raums, der mit dem Galeriegarten und dem Innenhof verbunden ist, freigemacht. Die klassischen Funktionen sind in verschiedene Unterzonen innerhalb des zentralen Raumes aufgeteilt und mit flexiblen Möbelinseln und integrierten Schränken ausgestattet, hinter denen sich ein Küchenarbeitsbereich, ein Frühstücksbereich mit Kleingeräten und eine Wein-/Bar-Ecke verbergen. Ein Regalsystem auf einer Seite des Raums enthält einen Schreibtisch mit einem Computer, während Doppelfenster mit Blick auf die Galerie für viel natürliches Licht und Belüftung in diesem Heimbürobereich sorgen. Mit Sesseln von Carl Hansen und einem kleinen Tisch ausgestattet, kann dieser Raum auf vielfältige Weise genutzt werden.

La remodelación de este apartamento de 97 m² en el barrio de Gràcia de Barcelona estuvo muy influenciada por el amor del propietario noruego por el diseño y la ciudad de Barcelona. Para conectar el interior con el espacio exterior y dejar entrar toda la luz posible, YLAB recuperó la galería original y liberó el interior creando un espacio central abierto en forma de L conectado con el jardín de la galería y el patio interior. Las funciones clásicas están segregadas en diferentes sub zonas dentro del espacio central y están amuebladas con islas de muebles flexibles y armarios integrados, que ocultan un espacio de trabajo en la cocina, una zona de desayuno con pequeños electrodomésticos y un rincón de vino/bar. Un sistema de estanterías en un lado del espacio contiene una zona de escritorio con un ordenador, mientras que las ventanas dobles que dan a la galería proporcionan mucha luz natural y ventilación a esta zona de oficina en casa. Amueblado con sillones Carl Hansen y una pequeña mesa, este espacio se puede utilizar de muchas maneras diferentes.

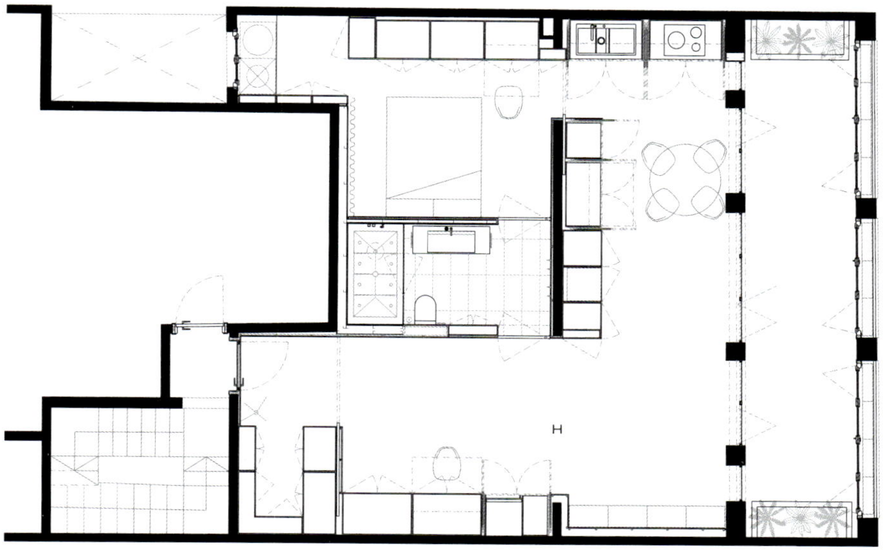

Floor plan